USE OF FORCE

Expert Guidance for Decisive Force Response

BRIAN A. KINNAIRD

Looseleaf
Law Publications, Inc.

43-08 162nd Street
Flushing, NY 11358
www.LooseleafLaw.com
800-647-5547

Library of Congress Cataloging-in-Publication Data

Kinnaird, Brian A., 1973-
  Use of force : expert guidance for decisive force response / Brian A. Kinnaird.
      p. cm.
Includes index.
      ISBN 1-889031-64-X
  1. Police. 2. Police training. 3. Police administration. 4. Law
enforcement. 5. Police brutality. I. Title.
      HV7921.K557 2003
      363.2--dc21

                                                                                                2003006798

The author is sensitive to the need and importance of female participation in the police service.

It is only for ease of reading that the masculine pronoun is used herein.

Cover Design by *Sans Serif, Inc.*, Saline, Michigan

TABLE OF CONTENTS

Dedication

For

Marideth and Wesley

Acknowledgments

Many individuals contributed to this book, both directly and indirectly. I'd like to thank Looseleaf Law Publications, Inc. for awarding my book contract and their professional participation in assisting practitioners in the field of criminal justice.

First, I'd like to thank my colleague at Fort Hays State University, Dr. Robert Scott, for his mentoring, and friendship. A thank you also goes out to current and former members of the Ellis County Sheriff's Department, Hays Police Department and Kansas Highway Patrol for their camaraderie and for planting the seeds that became the foundation for a prosperous career in academia. Thanks also to Larry Lein and Chris Lein (Law Enforcement and Security Trainers, Inc.) for their insight into a unique world of use of force options.

A very special thanks goes out to my parents, Jerry and Patricia Kinnaird, for their support and love that has fostered the man I am today. My in-laws, Bill and Shirley Andrews, for their continuous advice, direction, and support. Most importantly, to my wife Marideth, who has lived with patience and fortitude throughout my graduate school and employment experiences, never once complaining about the choices I made.

I would also like to acknowledge the following individuals and organizations, for this book would not be possible without their help: Ed Nowicki, Jeff Chudwin, Joe Truncale, Greg Meyer, Michael P. Stone, John H. Lombardi and Associates, Calibre Press, Inc., Kansas Law Enforcement Training Center, and the Peace Officers Standards and Training Commission.

Finally, I wanted to acknowledge all law enforcement officers and criminal justice practitioners who risk their lives daily for the greater good of mankind and to those who are no longer with us that made the ultimate sacrifice in that same pursuit.

"Blessed are the peacemakers for they shall be called the Children of God."   Matthew 5:9

About the Author

Brian A. Kinnaird serves as the Director of Justice Studies at Fort Hays State University in Hays, KS. Professor Kinnaird is currently a candidate for a Ph.D. in the field of human services with an emphasis in criminal justice from Capella University (Minneapolis, MN). He received baccalaureate and master's degrees in the field of sociology and criminal justice from Fort Hays State University (Hays, KS). Professor Kinnaird is a former law enforcement officer and graduate of the 143rd Basic Training class at the Kansas Law Enforcement Training Center. He served as a corrections officer and deputy sheriff with the Ellis County Sheriff's Department (Hays, KS). He was assigned as lead defensive tactics trainer, was a member of the Special Situations Response Team (S.S.R.T.) and was also responsible for the field training of new recruits. Professor Kinnaird is an active member of the American Society for Law Enforcement Trainers and is a Policy Fellow with the Docking Institute of Public Affairs. He is published in a variety of outlets regarding use of force and police management and currently consults and trains officers in use of force principles and defensive tactics across the United States.

Foreword

Brian Kinnaird's "Use of Force" guide is long overdue. My last few years as a Special Agent with the FBI, I was assigned to investigate civil rights complaints against law enforcement officers. I observed firsthand some of the problems that law enforcement face when dealing with the public. In addition, I spent 23 years as a FBI Police Instructor dealing with use of force. This gave me a unique perspective on police use of force from both sides of the fence, so to speak.

Let's ask ourselves the question, "What area of law enforcement gets most officers and departments in trouble with the people with whom they come in contact?" USE OF FORCE UNDER COLOR OF LAW! When law schools are offering classes to attorneys on how to sue police, where do you think litigation is going in the 21st century?

Two things became obvious from my civil rights investigations. First, I found that most law enforcement officers did not understand the ramifications of their agency's use of force policy. If an officer does not understand that policy, how can he/she make sure not to violate it when using force? Second, I found that many departments wrote their use of force policy to protect themselves and not the officers that worked for them. An officer can act within the law, but still be out of policy! Where does that leave him/her? It opens the officer up for a civil suit against himself as an individual. I read one part of a department's use of force policy that went so far as to specify that the officer needed to determine the intent of a subject before the officer could know what level of force he could use!

From my 29 years of training law enforcement officers, the one thing that stands out about training and policy is that it must be simple and easy to understand. Officers are like most people; they will train and study hard while in a training atmosphere. However, once they leave that environment and the training and studying is left up to them as an individual, they don't do it! I get many questions that deal with use of force; specifically, how to know when to administer force and how much force to use. The courts have given us a map to plot our answers to those questions. Too many administrators have a tendency to make the answers too difficult and too technical to try and anticipate every situation an officer may encounter. When they write their use of force policy to cover every situation, the policies become too lengthy and difficult for the individual officer to understand and remember.

When I lecture to law enforcement officers about the "Practical and Legal Consideration in Use of Force Management", I stress simplicity and common sense. If you have a written policy that no one understands, or can remember, what value is it to your officer? It would seem that someone is trying to be very academic in a non-academic area, or is trying to write a comprehensive policy to protect the department. Either way, both approaches are wrong and do not bode well for officers. Department administrators do not always like to hear that the best asset to their departments are their own officers, and that they should try to protect them from being sued. This can easily be done by keeping their policies short, concise and based upon a common sense approach to make it easier for the officers to understand and adhere to in their actions.

Another recommendation that I make to administrators is to give the officers what I call "an officer discretion paragraph" in the policy. They should spend time, effort, and money in the continuous training of their officers, so why not let them use their "discretion", based on that training in their use of force. It is much easier than having someone try to write a policy that covers every conceivable situation an officer may encounter that requires the application of force.

Most use of force policies that I have observed, deal with a generic officer and subject. If the subject does this, then the officer can respond with that application of force. Wrong! If the officer is 5' 2", 115 pounds and the subject is 6' 2", 260 pounds, is that officer restricted to the same use of force that a 6' 2", 260-pound officer uses in dealing with a 5'2", 115-pound subject? If your policy does not allow different responses in different situations it is detrimental to your officers and thus to your department. That is why I proposed the Common Sense Use of Force Model and is presented in this book.

What is reasonable force? This is probably the most asked question in law enforcement training when dealing with use of force today. My definition of *reasonable force* is, **that force the officer, by necessity, needs to use in order to gain control and maintain control of a subject, or defend a life, based on the common sense factors and any training the officer has received**. "By necessity" will vary depending on the common sense factors that are present for a given situation. "Any training the officer has received" will cover an officer that may have received training in a technique or procedure that is not currently approved by his present employer. In today's world, many officers start out in one department and later transfer to another. Should that officer be penalized if, in a high stress situation, they revert back to a technique in which their previous employer trained them? I don't think so. However, many departments' use of force policies do not allow that previously learned use of force.

In this text, Professor Kinnaird is also concerned with training for law enforcement officers. Each time you read an article about control tactics training, what does the author say? It has to be easy to learn, easy to use, easy to retain and effective. As Bruce K. Siddle stated in his book *Sharpening The Warrior's Edge,* "the ideal survival skill should be kept as simple as possible in technique complexity, technique response time, and theory of application." Mr. Siddle also quoted a study that found, "that as the number of response options (techniques) increased from one to two, reaction time increased by 58%." Going into the 21st century, officers need to move away from thinking of defensive tactics and start thinking towards control tactics. That is what law enforcement officers do. They are proactive in controlling subjects and, initially, do not need to defend themselves from a subject if they are successful in their control of that subject. One of the control tactics programs that Professor Kinnaird talks about in his book is the Chris Lein Arm Management Program (CLAMP). This program is one to take into the 21st century. It is not in competition with any other training but rather complements training and meets all of the requirements outlined by Mr. Siddle. Yes, self-defense tactics also are needed in any training program.

Another area in which law enforcement agencies and officers can help themselves is that of report writing. One simple adjustment in reporting the use of force is to change the name of the report. Instead of calling the report a "police use of force report", rename it a "subject resistance report." The same information can be collected in the report, but it gives a different connotation to a jury. It transfers the cause of the use of force to the subject's actions instead of the initiative of the police officer.

If police officers and administrators can adhere to the principles discussed in this book, then the best is yet to come. The 21st century in law enforcement can be a great one for the individual officer if, in their use of force in dealing with the public, they keep the following as a guide: Use common sense in the use of force and be morally right, ethically right, and tactically right!

Larry E. Lein
FBI Special Agent (Ret.)
President, Law Enforcement
& Security Trainers, Inc.

Introduction

This book is a culmination of training, education, and experience in a critical and everyday phenomenon in criminal justice service: use of force. While law enforcement officers, by virtue of their duty, most often use force; many other individuals in the field use force as well. Therefore, the rhetoric "criminal justice practitioners" is often used throughout this book as a need to address all members of the criminal justice community who have the option to use force in the scope of their duties. Law enforcement, corrections, probation and parole, juvenile justice, and private security at every level of government are all entities that comprise this community.

A fascinating part of work in the criminal justice field are "war stories" that are told. In the office, at the doughnut shop, during mealtime, at home and at parties, are all places where practitioners share experiences both funny and not so funny. As a law enforcement officer, I've had the opportunity to participate in these stories that are explicit displays of courage, camaraderie, empathy and tenderness as well as ignorance and deviance. Most significant to me, have been the stories of law enforcement officers who have engaged in serious situations where force was used by or against a violator. In all of these incidences, questions about force were raised, fears became situated in these questions and decisions were made. Talk to any cop and they will tell you a time where they were subject to the "pucker factor" as a result of a use of force response. The uncomfortableness and uneasiness that goes along with incidences of force are undeniable. Consequently, it has been the goal of many researchers and trainers in the human service disciplines to quell some of these tensions and provide some insight in an effort to make use of force responses, and aspects of decision-making, a positive experience for criminal justice professionals.

It wasn't until an evening traffic stop on a lone interstate in western Kansas that it became my goal as well. An intoxicated subject westbound on I-70 finally pulled over for me after a three-mile pursuit. It was apparent in his intoxicated state that the offender had not seen my lights nor heard my sirens during this time. I did not have immediate backup but knew officers were enroute to my location (it is not uncommon for rural officers to be the only ones on-duty or to have their backup literally minutes away). Following a brief DUI field investigation that led to his arrest, the subject "decided" he wasn't going to jail. Having put on the first handcuff, the fight was on. During this three-minute incident that seemed like a lifetime, I was losing. A drunken man three times my age and without a clue what to do next was over-powering me. How could this be? *I* was the one with the knowledge. *I* was the law enforcement officer. What was happening? Luckily, my backup finally arrived and the arrest was made successfully and without further incident. Going home later that night it hit me...what if? What if my backup had not arrived in time? What if I couldn't have stopped the attack on my person? I felt stripped of all my authority. For the first time it dawned on me that I may not have gone home. I felt weak and was inconsolable for some time.

The situation that beckoned my service was just one of the many incidences in police duty that have and will occur forever. What does *not* have to occur, however, is indecisiveness and the feelings of inadequacy when using or responding to force. I found that many officers before and after me have shared in these same experiences and feelings. Whether using a firearm or handcuffs, the use of force is an awesome power bestowed upon criminal justice practitioners. It follows that a commensurate fostering of skills, knowledge, attitudes, and belief systems, will assist in governing the proper use of force while effectively conducting police duty.

This book is a collectivity of years of research and experience regarding the use of force in criminal justice. It is designed as an academy or in-service training reference, administrative guide or as academic and training literature for use of force instructors. It contains topics based upon academic literature reviews, contemporary research, and field experiences. It also provides theories and models applicable in use of force decision-making, policy and procedure, litigation, and training. I will have achieved my goal if law enforcement administrators, trainers, and officers close this book and have a better understanding of the implications that surround a complicated aspect of criminal justice duty: use of force.

Brian A. Kinnaird

Chapter 1 – Background

HISTORY OF FORCE

In accomplishing police objectives, officers are given great power and authority. The use of force is the most significant display of authority and control that all law enforcement officers possess. The type and amount of force that can be used, however, depends on exercising sound judgment and competence in accordance with legal guidelines and department policy. Before analyzing the purposes and goals of the use of force, it is appropriate to provide some historical contexts of force as a foundation upon which contemporary laws and ethical practices are observed.

Throughout history, the use of force in punishment and crime control took many forms. The American experience with policing paralleled that of Europe, thus the criminal justice system developed from similar contexts during each period. Prior to formal, written codes of law and morality, it was the responsibility of the public to impose punishment for offenders. Through various force options from stoning during the biblical period (3000 B.C. to A.D. 500) to blood feuds during the medieval era (A.D. 500-1000), victims had sole discretion in carrying out punishment mechanisms (Hemmens, 1999). Newman (1985) suggested that these were practiced as "non-legal" initiatives long before the legal use of force was ever developed.

From the Middle Ages to the late 1600s, however, control and punishment became more formalized. Procedures developed for using force against offenders that made punishment less erratic. At the time, both the church and state maintained authority over separate domains of criminality (Hemmens, 1999). Following a breakdown of belief systems regarding religion and political power as congruent and reciprocal elements of governance, the church and state separated. Subsequently, the notion of individual rights and "social contracts" gained momentum. John Locke gave rise to this perspective, explaining that the authority to govern should be created between the government and the governed (Locke, 1980 [1690]). The state only existed, then, to protect the natural rights of citizens. Consequently, the state governed the imposition of the use of force in an attempt to prevent individuals from using it in ways that violated others' natural rights. Weber (1947) suggested that this philosophy developed into common law authority over the use of force in England. This, in turn, affected the rest of Western Europe and the United States regarding the acquisition of common law to control and punish deviant members of society.

During the early American period (1650-1830), policing and punishment remained public and corporal. As societies became more complex, a division of labor and lack of social solidarity illustrated that informal methods of using force and imposing punishment were ineffective. The watch system, implemented as a transitional model of order maintenance, did not satisfy the public. As a result, England's Sir Robert Peel organized an even more formal program of policing in 1829. Consisting of uniformed patrol divisions and investigative units, Peel sought to legitimize police operations including the use of force. Terrill (2001) provided that the United States mirrored Peel's organizational initiative with Boston's police agency in 1837. By the late 1800s, most cities in the United States had established police forces with formal operations including use of force options (Reid, 1988).

It wasn't until 1931 and the Wickersham Commission that the police use of force was brought to national attention. Unfortunately, brutality was the concept discussed in reports that illustrated police tactics as a major institutional problem (National Commission on Law Observance and Enforcement, 1931). It was determined that the police viewed force as a necessary measure for citizen compliance and also as a method of respect towards them as authority figures (Westley, 1953). By the 1960s, the police use of force was given considerable scholarly attention in respect to perceptions and tactics. During a period of civil unrest that saw rioting in response to police tactics, President Johnson's Law Enforcement Assistance Act (LEAA) was created to help eliminate the excessive uses of police force, most notably deadly force. With funding for better training and education, the commission sought to professionalize the criminal justice system by legitimizing the police institution in respect to its goals and tactics. What is quantitatively known about the police use of force has been discerned over a period of only 30 years, through research consisting mostly of observations, reports, and surveys. Furthermore, the research has emphasized the use of deadly force and to a much lesser degree, less-than-lethal and non-lethal force.

PURPOSE OF FORCE

Although the police have existed and continue to exist as the only institution to ensure that common laws are followed in society, Bittner (1970) argued that giving the right to the police to use coercive tactics goes against middle-class values in achieving peace. What he failed to recognize, however, is that all institutions in society require force by the police in order to achieve and maintain civilization. Ultimately, appropriate police tactics are determined by societal choices and *not* those made by the police. Subsequent to this phenomenon, Sherman (1980) provided a police officer's paradox when he noted that officers must use violence in order to stop violence.

Force is defined as "any bodily impact, restraint, or confinement or threat thereof" (Stetser, 2001, p. 17). The general rule used by all jurisdictions from state to state is that necessary force is the only lawful force when force options must be used. Furthermore, force is not measured by mechanism but by *manner*. The environment that is encountered by the law enforcement officer determines the manner in which force is used. Officers must be able to show capability, opportunity, and jeopardy when discerning force options. Did the violator have the capability, such as a weapon, to harm the officer or others? Did an opportunity exist for the violator to use the weapon? Was there a perceivable, imminent threat to the officer or others, warranting the use of force? Carter (2002) provided additional factors to be considered when assessing the need to use force. Was the suspect peacefully submitting or actively resisting? What was the nature and seriousness of the crime? Was there a previous arrest record that indicated a pattern of violence? Were the surrounding environmental conditions favorable or threatening?

EXTENT OF FORCE

Quantitative data on the use of force by police officers is generally lacking, as many agencies fail to administer use of force reporting forms or discern definitions of force as their personnel use them. Consequently, most quantifiable data has been derived from survey research of officer-citizen encounters. The National Institute of Justice, the Bureau of Justice Statistics, and the Bureau of the Census conducted such a survey during 1996. Greenfield (1996) provided data estimating that 44.6 million persons had face-to-face contact with officers during 1996. The most common reasons for contact included calls for assistance by the public, victim and witness crime reporting, and traffic accidents and citations. Interestingly, the public, and not the police officer, initiated most contacts. Furthermore, 1.2 million persons were handcuffed during 1996. Another 500,000 persons were hit, held, pushed, choked, threatened with a flashlight and chemical sprays or restrained by a police dog.

As a derivative of the 1994 Violent Crime Control and Law Enforcement Act, which required the Attorney General to determine the scope of excessive force by officers, the International Association of Chiefs of Police (IACP) Use of Force Report was created as a collectivity of data and standards based upon research and advisory boards. Federal funding of this project ceased in 1997 and the IACP continued the endeavor due to the significance of force in policing and the importance in data collection in providing knowledge acquisition for the development of training, policies and best practices. Although new data is being gathered as of this writing, findings on the extent of police force have officially been recorded in 1998 and 2000, explicitly illustrating that officers in limited numbers of situations use force.

In 1998, the IACP reported that officers used force 4.19 times per every 10,000 calls for service (see figure 1.1) while the 2000 report denoted only 3.5 instances of force per 10,000 calls for service (see figure 1.2) (IACP, 2001). Additionally, it was determined that force was employed most frequently in field arrest situations with physical force being the dominate force option followed by chemical force and firearms. Indeed, these numbers illustrate improvement and serve as positive feedback for administrators and officers alike. The cornerstone of such effectiveness in the reduction and maintenance of force incidences are attributed to appropriate leadership by law enforcement administrators, effective policy and quality continuous training.

Excessive force. The difficulty with using any type of force is determining the degree to which an officer can use it. Outside of what is considered "reasonably necessary" under statutory provisions is believed excessive by those same legal parameters. The excessive use of force is often difficult to define, as it is understood from many different contexts. Terrill (2001) provided that the excessive use of force is also called the use of excessive force, brutality, unauthorized force, wrongful force, and misuse of force. These terms are only interchangeable to some. Adams (1995) explained that the use of excessive force is the use of more force than is necessary to obtain offender compliance. The excessive use of force, however, could be using force too many times. Fyfe (1988) made similar distinctions between brutality and unnecessary force. While brutality can be understood as the deliberate and wrongful use of force, unnecessary force can be that level of force employed by officers that are ill-trained or equipped to handle an incident. In an article published by the International Association of Chiefs of Police (IACP) in 2001, it was reported that officers used excessive force in less than one-half of one percent of all force-employed incidences. Obviously, no amount of excessive force is acceptable in policy duty; however, this number explicitly puts into perspective the scope of excessiveness in quantifiable contexts. In other words, "cops do not use excessive force as much as they are reported to." Recently, the significance of civil litigation claims filed and negative media attention have thrust law enforcement into a frenzy of assessment initiatives and accountability measures that have also ultimately increased anxiety, frustration, and sick leave while decreasing budgets, personnel and morale. While

assessment serves as a benchmark in illustrating true effectiveness of law enforcement officers in responding to force, it also
answers questions and provides such data as listed above.
Although it is appropriate and necessary to continuously plan
and assess for the future, take a moment to study the numbers
provided above in reference to excessive force. Once in a great
while, one must stop to "smell the roses" and indeed, the
reduction in numbers above provides somewhat of a fragrance.

FIGURE 1.1

RATE OF POLICE USE OF FORCE PER 10,000 CALLS-FOR-SERVICE BY JURISDICTIONAL SIZE

1998

Population Group	Other	Physical	Chemical	Electronic	Impact	Firearm	Totals
1	0.00	1.39	0.72	0.00	0.14	0.00	**2.25**
2	0.00	6.27	0.81	0.00	0.35	0.17	**7.60**
3	0.00	3.11	1.07	0.00	0.54	0.11	**4.83**
4	0.00	0.00	2.08	0.00	0.00	0.00	**2.08**
5	0.00	0.00	0.00	0.00	0.00	2.75	**2.75**
6	0.00	2.18	2.94	0.00	0.25	0.12	**5.49**
7	0.00	0.00	0.00	0.00	0.00	0.00	**0.00**
8	0.00	5.59	2.90	0.00	0.38	0.05	**8.92**

Note: This report examines incidents of use of force by police officers. It uses the highest degree of force by each officer involved in an incident to determine the rankings.

POPULATION GROUP LEGEND

Group	Range
1	0-15,000
2	15,001-35,000
3	35,001-55,000
4	55,001-85,000
5	85,001-170,000
6	170,001-500,000
7	500,001-1,000,000
8	1,000,001-99,999,999

FIGURE 1.2
RATE OF POLICE USE OF FORCE PER 10,000 CALLS-FOR-SERVICE BY JURISDICTIONAL SIZE
2000

Population Group	Other	Physical	Chemical	Electronic	Impact	Firearm	Totals
1	0.00	1.31	0.27	0.00	0.03	0.03	**1.64**
2	0.00	0.86	0.95	0.00	0.17	0.34	**2.32**
3	0.00	0.00	0.00	0.00	0.00	1.04	**1.04**
4	0.00	0.00	0.00	0.00	0.00	0.00	**0.00**
5	0.00	0.00	0.00	0.00	0.30	0.00	**0.30**
6	0.00	0.00	0.00	0.00	0.00	0.00	**0.00**
7	0.00	0.00	0.00	0.00	0.00	0.00	**0.00**
8	0.00	0.00	0.00	0.00	0.00	0.00	**0.00**

Note: This report examines incidents of use of force by police officers. It uses the highest degree of force by each officer involved in an incident to determine the rankings.

POPULATION GROUP LEGEND

Group	Range
1	0-15,000
2	15,001-35,000
3	35,001-55,000
4	55,001-85,000
5	85,001-170,000
6	170,001-500,000
7	500,001-1,000,000
8	1,000,001-99,999,999

ETHICS AND POLICING

The changing face of crime and deviance in America has necessitated a unique response in dealing with crime control. Consequently, law enforcement agencies, as human service components, have changed their prescription regarding autonomous police duty. Current trends focus on such elements as officer-partner relationships, patrolling techniques and specialized skill units to better achieve amelioration in police duty. From bicycle patrols to paramilitary police units, specialized task forces currently serve as efficacious police responses to situations that normal patrol officers are often ill-prepared to handle. Although academy instruction, in-service, and departmental field training function as the backbone of professional, service-oriented law enforcement, it is naive to assume that an individual officer possesses all of the skills necessary to meet every aspect of crime and deviance that threatens society. Furthermore, one cannot simply associate one particular police response based upon a mutually exclusive perspective of crime and its demographics.

As most often illustrated, through such events as the Rodney King beating in Los Angeles, the Diallo shooting, the Louima brutalization in New York City, and the coverage of school violence that has swept America, law enforcement agencies are now more than ever under a watchful eye in respect to preparation and proficiency in justice administration. In particular, the use of force as a tool for the control and safety of the public-at-large is under scrutiny and has been for some time. Between the lack of understanding of its operational implications by the public and the use and misuse of that force by those sworn to serve and protect, the use of force is a police response that is criticized and subject to constant litigation. Designed to be a simple, comprehensive and pragmatic application for justice system constituents, the federal use of force continuum offers a dynamic force response to a dynamic criminal environment. Because of the changing face of policing to meet contemporary threats in society, ambiguities cloud the applicability of this force continuum. Is the use of force the same for both female and male officers? Do tactical teams, i.e., S.W.A.T., S.O.R.T., etc. apply force through the same methods observed by foot patrols? What is considered "less-than-lethal" force? Do service of drug warrants require different force responses than those needed in serving tax warrants? What are the implications of force for those police units that wear battle dress uniforms as compared to the civilian attire worn by criminal investigators? Or the correctional officer working in a semi-controlled environment? Outside of the practicality of use of force models, which are primarily motivated by legal parameters, ethical considerations must be given in responding to criminal and non-criminal environments.

No single tool of police operations is as visible or important as the use of force. The primary responsibility of any law enforcement agency is to provide security, protection, and service to the citizens of their community. While many entities comprise the criminal justice system, it is the police patrol function where most citizen-police encounters take place. Ill-trained or poorly equipped officers easily destroy years of good police-community relations by improper uses of force. Conversely, properly trained and equipped officers give their community confidence in their ability to achieve police duty, working as true professionals.

Police professionalism. To whom does society bestow the title "professional?" Can any group or individual be considered a professional by the mere fact that they are gainfully employed? Generally, professionals possess characteristics that make their work honorable, such as perfected skills, crafts, or arts. As a result, doctors, lawyers, and educators enjoy a professional status through blind faith ability given to them by the general public. Nichols (2001) explained that it is not uncommon to hear people exclaim, "That's my doctor", "my lawyer", or "my teacher." Few people, however, say, "That's my cop!" Similarly, Murphy (2001) argued that policing is the "unprofessional profession." Consider that such justice system members like police and correctional officers possess powers of authority and discretion that is often associated with a profession but they are not given the respect and autonomy that professionals enjoy. He further explained that the biggest problem with many criminal justice systems becoming professional is the failure of proper support structures. "The most fundamental weakness in crime control is the failure of federal and state governments to create a framework for local policing" (Murphy, 1989, p. 3). Consequently, over 17,000 local departments become the victims of a fragmented, unworkable, non-system. While efforts are being made in contemporary police society to attain professional status, officers remain cynical and frustrated by irrational management and illogical variations in policies and procedures (Murphy, 1989). Additional problems arise when poorly motivated officers become deviant and succumb to laziness and mediocrity promulgated by poor management and leadership. For the faithful service of justice, criminal justice members comprising the areas of police, courts, and corrections must participate in a similar system of standards in an effort to achieve effective crime control.

In being concerned with human behavior, human service agents must also be concerned with ethical behavior. Right and wrong actions in conjunction with normative values become the yardstick for officer judgments. Because laws are codified by morals and values of any given society, law and ethics are inextricably linked. In developing ethics, however, the fact must be accepted that officer behavior is not always consistent with laws and policies. Regardless, an officer's behavior is not without moral implications. Questions must be asked in respect to ethics and policing. What is the excellence of character and is a formal code of ethics only a symbolic expression or does it truly guide decision-making?

Excellence of character. In determining police behavior that eventually leads to use of force decision-making, an understanding of human character is of integral importance in defining ethical behavior that governs decision-making.

Individuals in society are not born into formed character. Despite arguments into the scope of biology and background as formative elements of ethical behavior, each human has a quality of ignorance that they are born and often die with. Delattre (2002) explained that in looking at the character of police officers, one must initially look at what is called the *first nature*. Crying behaviors of babies, for example, elicit sympathetic and immediate responses to their needs. Curiousness and responsiveness is also evident when babies cry as a result of another crying baby. In addition to impulsiveness, Delattre (2002) provided that at this age we are indifferent to our demands on others. "We have yet to develop a sense of self; our character remains to be formed" (p. 6).

In comparison to our first nature, *second nature* encompasses the traits individuals acquire as a result of training and learned responses that ultimately form habits and dispositions. Essentially, babies are born with no evidence of character. If one is born into ignorance of moral ideals, it is the instruction and training that assists in achieving a second nature. "If we are normal human beings, and not incapacitated by some abnormal defect, then whether we acquire a good or bad character depends on the kind of upbringing we get" (Urmson, 1988, p. 25). Burnyeat (1980) further substantiated habit as a second nature, as he exclaimed that it is inevitable that one responds and acts upon what is natural for them. The excellence of character, then, depends heavily on the second nature of human beings.

The social climate is not the sole contributor to the development of good character. Most feelings, judgments, or actions rely upon self-discipline and self-reflection in *wanting* to become a good person. This task is most difficult for adults, who have the propensity to serve already established bad habits and who often lack the discipline or aspiration to change. As an athletic analogy, consider the golf swing. It is much easier to master when one has not already developed bad habits in respect to that swing. Comparatively, moral habits are acquired and sustained through appropriate training at an early age. This comparison of ideals is not a new paradigm. Aristotle observed that "people's characters take their bias from the steady directions of their activities...it is these persistent activities in certain directions that make them what they are" (Burnyeat, 1980, p. 86).

It is not difficult to assume that all criminal justice agencies want to recruit candidates of sound moral character. A poignant question can be raised, however, regarding the understanding of that character. How is it defined and is it explicitly or implicitly understood?

In 1980, a Miami police department recruited 200 individuals, 80 percent of this population consisting of minority residents (Delattre, 2002). Despite questionable backgrounds, these police recruits were sent to the academy and returned only to be subject to poor field training and inadequate supervision. Ultimately, the Internal Affairs Division permitted the new officers to function within a deviant police social structure. More than one third of these recruits had been fired by 1988 and twelve of these so called "meat eaters" had been convicted of crimes from drug trafficking to murder (Thompson, 1988). Ineffective or non-existent codes and standards provided the foundation for deviant and unethical behavior by these officers. The propensity to identify these individuals as unethical could have been determined beforehand through appropriate background investigations, academy instruction assessments and subsequent field training.

By comparison, "grass eaters," as a construct of unethical police character, are semi-controlled individuals who rarely trust themselves during times of deviant opportunity. They may simply give in to temptations during times of stress or succumb to their weak will. McAlary (1987) provided that these individuals rationalize their conduct through the excuse that "others do it."

Regardless of the context of police character, officers reveal their behavioral traits at some point in their recruitment or active duty. The environment in which their character is revealed is problematic, as it may depend upon the situation before they exhibit certain ethical or unethical behavior patterns. Delattre (2002) further explained that, "A police officer's fitness to wear the badge depends on the acquisition of habits of just behavior" (p. 11). Consequently, *just* officers can discern the difference between expending energy to the public for the sake of gratuities and serving the public interest with that same energy with little to no expectation of a return. Additionally, justice-oriented officers exercise discretion appropriately and do not abuse their power. Ker Muir (1977) argued that good police officers should understand human suffering as well as respect for justice, and using coercive tactics to achieve it.

Delattre (2002) provided two aspects of significant importance regarding the excellent character of police officers: balanced perception and integrity. The first aspect contemplates making the best of circumstances in volatile and ambiguous situations. Consider, for example, a domestic violence call. Police officers must be able to end the violence perpetrated and restore order to the scene, all while exercising compassion, honesty, and respect for the parties involved. Understanding how all of these factors are related helps eliminate the potential for conflict in respect to officer judgments during the situation.

Delattre (2002) explained integrity as analogous to the homogenization of milk. It is only with the capacity of wholeness that one can satisfy such excellence of character. Is an officer of integrity the same individual both in private and public life? Ethically, behavior and actions are to be the same in public and private respectively. This premise is conflicting, however, with contemporary ideals in general society. Today, it is not uncommon to understand one's personal and professional lifestyle as existing on separate planes, adhering to different principles of conduct. Can it not be said, though, that the life of a person makes all life personal? Despite contrasting dimensions of life, it exists within one individual. Kooken (1957) explained, "Habits that are formed in the home and among working associates are reflected in a policeman's relations with the public...One cannot be a gentleman in public and a cad in private" (p. 21). Delattre (2002) added that simply being one thing through and through is not the essence of character. Terrorists function similarly in public and private life yet these individuals do not exhibit what one would constitute as "integrity." A simple test of integrity is perhaps best characterized in Plato's *The Republic*. Much like the magical ring that allowed the wearer to become invisible, how would one truly behave if granted such power?

Ethical codes. As the ultimate purveyor of police profession-alism, the traditional "Law Enforcement Code of Ethics" published by the International Association of Chiefs of Police (IACP) provides a congruent set of principles that promote ethical behavior for sworn law enforcement officers. Although this code is explicitly understood when police officers are commissioned, many officers complain that the code is either ambiguous or too demanding. Within the context of these principles, such action verbs as "serve," "safeguard," "respect," and "protect" suggest that certain specialties be required in order to provide fundamental duties. To accept this role, officers must dedicate their lives in *pursuit* of such fundamentals. In doing so, it is required that police duty be served within the scope of due process of law. Unfortunately, this places officers into an uncomfortable position, as they must protect the civil rights and liberties of those who choose to commit illegal acts (Nichols, 2001). "They point to the great difficulty—or impossibility—of safeguarding lives and protecting the innocent from deception, and the weak from intimidation and simultaneously acting within the laws in respecting everyone's right to privacy and liberty" (Delattre, 2002, p. 31).

The second paragraph of the code explains that officers should set an example for others. As mentioned previously, this is where behavior in both public and private life come into contention. Constantly scrutinized by the public, officers must enforce the law while obeying those same laws in the scope of their duties. If the police are to cite those not wearing safety belts while operating a motor vehicle, is it not illegal for officers to fail wearing theirs? Furthermore, this behavior is unethical, as officers are to be exemplary in the course of their daily police functions.

Ethical law enforcement officers must also act officiously and not accept gratuities. The all too often-used phrase, "That badge and gun don't make you right!" uttered by John Q. Citizen is only half-correct, for the badge and gun does not give officers the right to think, feel, and act as if they are *better* than anyone else or that they can act *above* the law. Citizens often fail to recognize that officers are public servants, servants to them, through the symbol of that badge and gun. Ultimately, behavior is governed by respect through reciprocal relationships between the police and public.

In accepting gratuities, law enforcement officers receive goods in exchange for services. It may be looking the other way in respect to traffic infractions or receiving free coffee in exchange for being visible to deter potential crime. While Nichols (2001) explained that many officers banter about the true nature of a free cup of coffee, perhaps the best answer regarding gratuity is decided in the expectation of police service. Surely restaurant owners can encourage officers to frequent their establishment without offering free drinks and discounts. In all actuality, most officers come to expect such courtesy from their community counterparts as a show of respect and a job well done. Unfortunately, the waitress who works under this auspice in exchange for a "get out of jail free card" will become rather upset when an officer, who does not frequent the establishment or exhibit gratuitous behavior, stops her.

In the last paragraph of the code of ethics, the police badge is denoted as a symbol of public faith. As an explicit and implicit display, the badge offers the public a symbol of professionalism. More than just stating your profession, however, one must strictly adhere to professional principles. "Once an officer becomes a pawn of crime, that officer aborts self-esteem, integrity, and the trust of the community. Such actions also affect other officers and the integrity of the agency" (Nichols, 2001, p. 9). In essence, the code of ethics provides that ideals should be weighed with tested judgment and wisdom of experience (Delattre, 2002). Consequently, the code is considered best as a general guideline for behavior, as it cannot take the place of wisdom and positive character. Much like the effects of policy and procedure, guidelines are indeed useful; however, codes of "ethics" do not necessarily motivate officers to behave appropriately. They actually have to *want* to.

Applied ethics. Pedagogical merit warrants the teaching of ethics in schools and colleges. Appropriate public service warrants the understanding of ethics by those who are hired to serve the public. Several types of ethics are currently taught in various schools of learning and to various groups of professionals. Descriptive ethics determine behaviors of individuals. Metaethics concentrates on constructs that discern morality such as defining "justice." Normative ethics focuses on reasoning processes regarding right and wrong decisions. By its nature, however, the function of ethics is practical (Carter, 2002). Applied ethics is more or less a typology of normative ethics in that it operationalizes decision-making and practical choices in a work setting.

Whether using force, writing reports or participating in new patrol strategies, law enforcement officers engage in ethical practices as an application. "Rather than contemplating a line of moral thought on a philosophical level, ethical questions are resolved through consideration of realistic outcomes of a decision" (Carter, 2002, p. 94). In respect to decision-making, its value is determined by a pragmatic exploration of ethical police duty. This is not to denigrate the importance or need of philosophical foundations, rather the perspective of such cases is utilitarian. What is the importance of applied ethics? Developing a reasoned approach to using discretion rather than decision-making habits encompasses a mixture of behaviors, attitudes, and occupational experiences that positively guide officers in the scope of police duty. The nature of the law enforcement profession allows autonomy and little oversight regarding decision-making. Consequently, ethical parameters provide a foundation for appropriate actions within the boundaries of the law.

Brown (1981) explained, "Police discretion is above all a behavioral process in which the interpretation of events and the choice of alternatives are strongly influenced by the values and beliefs of the actor" (p. 221). In maintaining integrity, these formal and informal value systems must be inculcated by police personnel. Wasserman (1988) provided that values are exhibited most explicitly through actions of the organization. Furthermore, Carter (2002) explained that decision-making criteria would be determined by an officer's experience within the context of subcultural ethics of policing. This includes those actions that are taken seriously as well as those that are viewed as irrelevant or inappropriate. Considering this perspective, it is critical for law enforcement agencies to promote a belief system that is proper in respect to standards of conduct. Pragmatically, values are adopted by leadership through value statements, policies, or by mere example. In addition to the organizational dynamics of ethics, many officers share the same values as those understood by their community counterparts. Consequently, their decision-making will not necessarily conform to the standard of "perfect justice" but it will adhere to the values of the community.

ETHICS AND FORCE

As mentioned previously, law enforcement officers are charged with the responsibility of enforcing the law while observing constraints on their own behavior. In doing so, different distinctions arise regarding legal behavior and ethical behavior. Sewell (2001) explained that such distinctions are particularly evident with deadly force. "In the parlance of a cop, a police shooting is either good or bad" (p. 186). A good shoot meets all applicable statutory laws and departmental guidelines; a bad shoot fails to meet any one of the two criteria. Within this context and from an ethical perspective, is deadly force the right thing to do? Is it the only way to handle a particular situation?

In other applications of force in the force continuum, additional questions must be asked. Is it reasonable and necessary based upon the totality of the circumstances? What is the purpose of the application: to punish, to threaten, to control? Is the likelihood of force options a result of officer conduct and demeanor? What is the scope of training, skill and experience relative to exercising force options?

Peak (1998) explained that uses of force fall under the definition of ethical dilemmas. Oftentimes situations are no-win in nature, with actions determined by an analysis of means and ends (Klockars, 1980). Is it true that uses of force can be legal and not ethical? Consider, for example, an emotionally disturbed person swinging a knife ten feet away from an officer. Deadly force is justified but the circumstances of the situation question the ethical premise of such force. Bittner (1999) explained that the true dilemma often falls within the parameters of physical security for both parties. Is deadly force the *last* resort? "Contrary to the word 'manhunt', humans may never be hunted and while a dangerous animal may be killed on sight, a dangerous person must be afforded the opportunity to yield" (Bittner, 1999, p. 2). No circumstances, including the mental and emotional state of the officer or suspect, should cloud the fact that the dangerous person is a human being. Despite behavior that denigrates their own humanity, a dangerous person must be handled objectively with the understanding that the force actions administered are not for the good of the person, rather it only expresses the moral integrity of the officer (Bittner, 1999).

Dirty Harry. In an article by University of Delaware criminal justice professor Carl Klockars, he wrote, "The Dirty Harry problem asks when and to what extent the morally good end warrants or justifies an ethically, politically, or legally dangerous means to its achievement" (Klockars, 1985, p. 55). In the film entitled *Dirty Harry*, a psychopathic killer kidnaps a young girl, buries her alive and then fails to provide information to her location after demanding and receiving a ransom. Clint Eastwood's character, Inspector Harry Callahan, illegally searches the suspect's room, identifies him as the abductor and then proceeds to track him down. Upon locating the suspect, Callahan shoots him in the leg and then stands on it, torturing the suspect until he discloses the girl's whereabouts. And although the girl is dead, the suspect is exonerated following the illegal search and confession. In this situation, Klockars (1985) explained that the problem was not what Dirty Harry *should* have done, rather he believed that most people would have wanted Harry to do something dirty. In fact, most audiences were thoroughly satisfied with Callahan's behavior and approved of his tactics despite the subsequent results. To what extent, however, does moral courage and sensitivity by police officers cross the line?

Clint Eastwood's character was justified in his actions by the goodness of purpose. A possibility that the victim was still alive in conjunction with the failure to provide information defined this premise. Criminal investigators typically use the sliding scale of criminal culpability to gain a suspect's confidence in eliciting a confession. Dirty Harry went from asking a question at gunpoint to torture. Ultimately, the excessive nature of his force questioned the foundation of moral integrity and necessity found most commonly in the slippery slope argument. Klockars (1985) further explained, "The troublesome issue in the Dirty Harry problem is not whether a right choice can be made, but that the choice must always be between two wrongs. And in choosing to do either wrong, the police officer inevitably taints or tarnishes himself" (p. 56). Delattre (2002) argued that the incompatibility of one moral theory over another taints no one. The officer, in fact, acts in accordance with a moral theory, both of which are seen with a measure of rightness and thus forces a decision between them.

Fatalism. In respect to the use of force and police conduct following the Rodney King incident of the early 1990s, responses from the public, police administrators, and academics have varied. In particular, one argument has stood out among the rest, both used and criticized frequently. A fatalism argument purports that law enforcement agencies are only microcosms of the larger society. "Since the general public includes a great range of excellence, mediocrity, and depravity, every police department must be expected to include the same characteristics" (Delattre, 2002, p. 217). A social systems perspective illustrates that societal ills are fostered in exchange relationships and influence individual and group behavior. If the broader society consists of brutality, incompetence, and a plethora of other illicit behaviors, the microcosm argument provides that the attitudes and misconduct will proportionately make its way into law enforcement agencies as well. Delattre (2002) explained that it is common to understand the beating of Rodney King through this premise. As with any explanation, however, problems arise in respect to its validity.

Fatalism within the microcosm context is a favored argument, as it forces solutions to problems beyond society's reach, thus sparing anyone responsibility. Furthermore, it is assumed that people are "born" into a society, neither group selecting one another (Delattre, 2002). *Trop v. Dulles* (1958) provided that no one can be denied citizenship into the United States as punishment for a crime. Therefore, it is a violation of the Eighth Amendment to deprive citizenship based upon certain circumstances. In law enforcement agencies, however, there is no membership right by virtue of birth and is irrespective of criminal misconduct.

Individuals "born" into a society need not be eligible, submit to standards, complete training programs, serve under probationary terms, and adhere to departmental policies. Police officers do. Law enforcement agencies are selective, therefore elevating its personnel above general, social norms (Delattre, 2002). Consequently, how can a selective social institution be considered a microcosm of a larger, non-selective society? As a selective institution, law enforcement agencies establish and implement principles for service. The officers who beat Rodney King were merely following principles for service as set forth by their administration and were ultimately acquitted of criminal wrongdoing as a result of those findings. They were not microcosms of a brutal, angry, and racially motivated society or department. They were selected candidates within a selective social institution and therefore the responsibility for the violations that were civil and ethical fell back on the agency itself, not so much the individuals.

Still, law enforcement agencies are not free from the influences of society around them nor can they be expected to completely screen out unfit applicants or eliminate all wrongdoing. The realistic goal is to minimize adverse social conditions through selective recruitment, training, and leadership. The ethical use of force is a culmination of this process and it is these variables that ultimately assure continuous quality improvement in the organization.

ASSURING ETHICAL CONDUCT

The ethical use of force by the police must be a sustained effort across law enforcement organizations. In promulgating this philosophy, how is it assured that officers will not only *use* force but that they will use it in an ethical and legal manner? How is it assured that the organization will provide a foundation of ethical standards for which officers may have a benchmark for successful police practice? The implications of force in policing require such questions to be answered and are most effectively achieved through the creation and maintenance of an ethical organizational environment. "Organizational culture—an organization's past and present influences, beliefs, myths, and patterns of behavior—is powerful in shaping member behavior and is itself open to being shaped by its members and by its leaders" (Braunstein and Tyre, 1999, p. 124). Recognition by the police of the need for binding limits is essential to their ethical conduct in the use of force. Specific areas of organizational culture are of integral importance in establishing ethical and legal police practices.

Selection

Although the organizational culture and value system provides the framework for the ethical use of force, the individuals who comprise that institution provide the foundation. For that reason, the selection of personnel is critical for organizational success (Sewell, 2001). Outside of general selection procedures including written and oral examinations, physical and psychological evaluations, and drug screenings, the most important factor in personnel selection is an extensive background investigation. Sewell (2001) recognized that the best predictors of future actions are past behaviors. He further explained that prior employment and personal history assist in examining the nature of work ethic, maturity, and the propensity for violence or aggressive behavior. Consequently, efforts must concentrate on hiring the most prepared candidates that exhibit ethical prowess and maturity. The Report of the Independent Commission on the Los Angeles Police Department (1991) substantiated the fact, however, that the selection process is not a cure-all for problems with behavior that lead to unethical uses of force. Rather, behavior is modified once an individual has begun work as a police officer. "Officers may enter the force well suited psychologically for the job, but may suffer from burnout, alcohol-related problems, cynicism, or disenchantment, all of which can result in poor control over their behavior" (p. xvi).

Training

As with any profession, police training serves as a foundation of knowledge acquisition at all levels of employment from candidacy to retirement. It reinforces value systems as understood by the organization and provides contemporary information based upon past practices. Most importantly, it satisfies the needs of police officers in respect to theories and practices of appropriate police duty.

Recruit

Recruit training, derived from the police academy, is required by state law for all entry-level law enforcement officers and some correctional officers. As part of the curriculum, this initial training exposes new recruits to laws, policies, and skills in use of force applications. Officer-candidates are also evaluated on their knowledge acquisition of those applications. Theories, modalities, and laws regarding tactics and proficiency are all encompassing force implications that have been at the core of police training efforts for years. Sewell (2001) explained that in recent years, training in the use of deadly force has expanded with the implementation of firearm simulation technology that provides real life scenarios for decision-making proficiency. Secondly, training in the ethics of force situations further expands the decision-making process. For example, when is force morally appropriate? What value does the law enforcement agency place on human life? What is the role of the police regarding service and protection? Bittner (1999) emphasized, "The rule here is that whatever a situation may seem to demand and however it develops, police officers' actions are limited by respect for the humanity of the people involved" (p. 2).

Field

Despite the training that an officer receives at the police academy, the field-training component is often heralded as the most significant. It is at this level that the recruit becomes aware and involved in the procedures, applications, and philosophies of the specific agency they work for. The officer becomes governed by a different body and is now outside of the classroom, on the street, and working in an autonomous capacity. It is for this reason that field-training programs be a structured system of learning that reflects agency directives and values specific to ethical tactics necessary for effective police duty.

In-service

The last training component emphasizes the continuing education of officers after their initial recruit and field training experience. Much like educators, who receive a certain number of in-service training hours each year for their certification, law enforcement officers undertake mandatory retraining for, among other things, the continued proficiency in skills and decision-making in the use of force. Having entered the police subculture following recruit and field training, it is imperative that officers be reminded and tested through training that congruent standards remain in effect regarding the ethics and purposes of force options. Furthermore, contemporary skills and tactics are introduced not only to promote the same ethical agenda but also to increase the proficiency and safety of officers when implementing force options.

Supervision

Skolnick and Fyfe (1993) explained that the propensity for illegal and unethical uses of force follow poor supervision or the involvement of superiors in such inappropriate practices. In many instances, supervisors are rewarded for force options that are out of line with professional policing tenets (Sewell, 2001). Once again, the need is placed upon strong organizational culture that promotes ethical behavior and provides strong leadership behind this mission. In response to the discrepancies between supervisors and line officers, all parties should be handled commensurate with ethical and legal guidelines. Therefore, any rewards or promotions should reflect the ethical organizational culture observed by all. Furthermore, administrators and their subordinates should have a congruent understanding of the implications that govern their use of force in the context of police practices. Administrators must express the goals and purposes of the agency's mission, follow those principles, and stand behind the decisions and actions of their officers. In assuring such ethical conduct applicable to the use of force, Delattre (1992) provided that officers "need to witness integrity in the *de facto* policies and practices of police departments and in the vitality of those policies as they are embodied in individual police" (p. 26). In essence, reciprocity must exist regarding the respect for decency from the institution and those individuals and groups that the institution produces.

Summary

With efforts to provide a safe and secure environment for society, law enforcement officers are vested with the legal authority to use force. The legitimate authority to use coercive tactics has existed for centuries. Force was historically used to punish those convicted of crimes in an effort to deter those "would be" offenders. With the rise in crime with population following the 19th century, use of force by the state became a formal practice and conducted as a means to *control* offenders more than as a means of punishment. The early to mid-twentieth century offered initiatives to make the police use of force similar across a body of law enforcement and "professional" in terms of application. That authority is guided by numerous variables, many of which conflict with one another within the larger contexts of the police culture but which also strive for uniformity across those same boundaries. Laws, court decisions, agency policies, training, and environmental circumstances all guide a law enforcement officer's use of force. Most importantly, personal and professional ethics exist as a foundation for which the application of force may be weighed.

While ethical standards regarding force are incorporated into both the organization and individual by a number of ways, each influences the other. At the core are the values and belief systems about who the police are what their role is and how general, ethical conduct governs the actions and behaviors of police personnel. The challenge given to every law enforcement agency is to make use of the ethically ideal as a *standard* of judgment. Officers and agencies that collectively steer by a beacon of proper decision-making and self-discipline ensure the ability to develop capacities that rise to the challenges that they will continue to face in the future. Furthermore, in judging use of police force, an examination is required of *the totality of the circumstances* in force incidences and not just those deemed as "excessive." One must also look beyond those quantifiable incidences of force and examine situations where force could have been used and was not. As a result, the lack of analysis in respect to the totality of the force circumstances provides little structure for assessing the use, misuse, or non-use of force.

Questions for Discussion

1. Discuss how the police use of force has changed since the 1931 Wickersham Commission Report. Are perceptions, belief systems, and tactics on force different today than those observed in 1931? How about 1961? Why or why not?

2. Define "force" and explain capability, opportunity, and jeopardy in discussing force options by law enforcement officers.

3. Explain why the use of force by law enforcement officers decreased from 1998 to 2000.

4. Discuss how celebrated use of force cases have necessitated an assessment of ethical law enforcement practices.

5. What is meant by the "Dirty Harry Syndrome?" Is "goodness of purpose" an appropriate justification for all use of force situations? Why or why not?

REFERENCES

Adams, K. (1995). Measuring the Prevalence of Police Abuse of Force. In William A. Geller and Hans Toch (Eds.), *And Justice for All: Understanding and Controlling Police Abuse of Force.* Washington, DC: Police Executive Research Forum.

Bittner, E. (1999). Ethical Dilemmas. *Subject to Debate, 13,* (11) p. 2.

Bittner, E. (1970). *The Functions of Police in Modern Society.* Washington, DC: Government Printing Office.

Braunstein, S., & Tyre, M. C. (1999). Are Ethical Problems in Policing a Function of Poor Organizational Communication? J. D. Sewell, *Controversial Issues in Policing.* Boston, MA: Allyn and Bacon, pp. 123-138.

Brown, M. (1981). *Working the Street.* New York: Russell Sage Foundation.

Burnyeat, M. F. (1980). Aristotle on Learning to Be Good. *Essays on Aristotle's Ethics.* Berkeley, CA: University of California Press.

Carter, D. L. (2002). *The Police and the Community* (7th ed.). Upper Saddle River, NJ: Prentice-Hall.

Delattre, E. J. (2002). *Character and Cops: Ethics in Policing* (4th ed.). Washington, DC: AEI Press.

Delattre, E. J., & Stripling, S. R. (1992). Police Integrity and Public Expectations. *The Public Interest Law Review.* Durham, NC: Carolina Academic Press.

Fyfe, J. J. (1988). *The Metro-Dade Police-Citizen Violence Reduction Project, Final Report, Executive Summary.* Washington, DC: Police Foundation.

Greenfield, L. A. (1996). *Police Use of Force: Collection of National Data.* Washington, DC: Government Printing Office.

Hemmens, C. (1999). *Use of Force: Current Practices and Policy.* Lanham, MD: American Correctional Association.

Independent Commission on the Los Angeles Police Department (1991). *Report of the Independent Commission on the Los Angeles Police Department.* Los Angeles, CA.

International Association of Chiefs of Police. (2001). *IACP Study Finds That Police Rarely Use Force* [On-line]. Available:
www.theiacp.org/pubinfo/pubs/162000useforce.htm

Ker Muir, W. (1977). *Police: Streetcorner Politicians.* Chicago, IL: University of Chicago Press.

Klockars, C. B. (1985). *The Idea of Police.* Chicago, IL: American Bar Foundation.

Klockars, C. B. (1980). The "Dirty Harry" problem. *The Annals of the American Academy of Political and Social Science, 452,* pp. 33-47.

Kooken, D. L. (1957). *Ethics in Police Service.* Springfield, IL: Charles C. Thomas.

Locke, J. (1980 [1690]). *Second Treatise of Civil Government.* Indianapolis, IN: Hackett.

McAlary, M. (1987). *The Buddy Boys: When Good Cops Turn Bad.* New York: G. P. Putnam and Sons.

Murphy, P. V. (2001). Foreword. In E. J. Delattre: *Character and Cops: Ethics in Policing* (4th ed.). Washington, DC: AEI Press.

Newman, G. (1985). *The Punishment Response*. Albany, NY: Harrow & Hester.

Nichols, L. D. (2001). *Law Enforcement Operations: Police Systems and Practices* (4th ed.). Richmond, CA: McCutchan.

Peak, K. J., Stitt, B. G., & Gleasor, R. W. (1998). Ethical Considerations in Community Policing and Problem Solving. *Police Quarterly, 1,* (3) pp. 19-34.

Reid, S. T. (1988). *Crime and Criminology*. New York: Holt, Rinehart & Winston.

Sewell, J. D. (2001). The Police Officer's Ethical Use of Force. Michael J. Palmiotto, *Police Misconduct: a Reader for the 21st Century*. Upper Saddle River, NJ: Prentice-Hall.

Sherman, L. W. (November, 1980). Perspectives on Police and Violence. *The Annals of the American Academy of Political and Social Science, 69,* pp. 69-100.

Skolnick, J. H., & Fyfe, J. J. (1993). *Above the Law: Police and the Excessive Use of Force*. New York: Free Press.

Stetser, M. (2001). *The Use of Force in Police Control of Violence*. New York: LFB Scholarly Publishing.

Terrill, W. (2001). *Police Coercion: Application of the Force Continuum*. New York: LFB Scholarly Publishing.

The National Commission on Law Observance and Enforcement (1931). *Report on Lawlessness in Law Enforcement*. Washington, DC: Government Printing Press.

Thompson, M. S. (February, 1988). *Miami Vice: Police Trafficking in Drugs*. Washington Post.

Urmson, J. D. (1988). *Aristotle's Ethics*. Oxford: Basil Blackwell.

Wasserman, R., & Moore, M. (1988). Values in Policing. *Perspectives in Policing*. Washington, DC: National Institute of Justice.

Weber, M. (1947). *The Theory of Social and Economic Organization*. New York: Free Press.

Westley, W. A. (1953). Violence and the Police. *American Journal of Sociology, 59,* pp. 34-41.

Chapter 2 – Risk Assessment

Traditionally, police responses have been concerned with threats in society that are external to the organization. Consequently, there is little attention given to the preparation for internal organizational threats. Police deviance and negligence of duty cannot be predicted in absolute terms; however, the potential is inherent in every officer. In 1950, the Federal Bureau of Investigation reported that there were 3.2 officers for every one crime (Lombardi, 1996). Today, there are 3.2 crimes for every one officer (Bennett, 1994). To compound this problem, it was reported that in 1991, 16 percent of job applicants were considered high risk, compared to 21 percent in 1992. Twenty-five percent of employees admitted to stealing from employers while 42 percent admitted being tempted to steal (Doyle, 1994). Additionally, administrators are failing to meet organizational needs, further introducing opportunities for deviance or negligence into the agency.

Considering internal threats, Fournies (1987) provided research addressing why subordinates have traditionally failed to follow operational procedures. In his study he found that most individuals did not know what the organizational objectives were, how to do them or why. Lombardi (1996) explained that when managers attempt to address the problem of nonperformance they often neglect the fact that employees have a lack of knowledge regarding their job duties. If police administrators fail to implement, communicate, or follow policy, officers will have no direction or will find little importance in following policy themselves. Control over the organization, then, becomes limited or non-existent. Over a period of time, this pattern may lead to non-random risks that perpetuate deviant or negligent opportunities. Failure to anticipate problems will ultimately create a reactive approach to organizational security instead of a proactive one. To protect police assets, consistently using the same management tools helps to reduce the opportunity for negligence in police use of force. This includes understanding organizational objectives, controlling through documentation, as well as implementing other risk reduction strategies. Defending a police organization against negligent operational claims can be difficult. Exploring policies and procedures and responding to specific defense queries comprise some of these difficulties. Understanding a strategy of defense litigation could actually help an agency organize evidence and define their position relative to the incident.

Elements of organizational dynamics provide the framework for the predatory prevention matrix as a social science model of proximate cause. This common sense application allows police administrators to learn from training and control through documentation so that deviant or negligent opportunity may be anticipated in terms of foreseeability. This matrix isolates four key variables in explaining or defending a police organization's proactive prevention efforts. They consist of policy, control, risk, and phases of attack (see figure 2.1). These are benchmark cells comprised of primary, secondary, and tertiary goals. Through this model, the primary goal is for police organizations to support and participate in intervention methods. The secondary goal of this model is for the organization to intervene before an incident occurs. It anticipates why officers need to follow policy, i.e., organizational goals and objectives. The tertiary goal is to reduce the probability of a criminal or negligent act being completed by the officer through effective control measures.

POLICY

In today's society, accountability is of integral importance in the police organization. As a result of criminal and civil litigations relative to police actions, law enforcement organizations are consistently inundated with accountability factors in an effort to improve police standards, control crime and serve the public. These factors are explicitly conveyed through certain tools and resources including training and education. Organizational policy, however, is the cornerstone of effective communication between the employer and employee in respect to identifying goals and operations within the organization. It also defines the first cell within the predatory prevention matrix.

Figure 2.1

The Predatory Prevention Matrix
BENCHMARK CELLS
(Rank order across columns do down rows)

4 Key Factors	Primary	Secondary	Tertiary
**POLICY (Static Definition of Problem)	**Policy**	**Objectives**	**Procedures**
	(What)	(Why)	(How)
**CONTROL (necessary documentation of proposed resolution of defined problem)	**Control**	**Patrol**	**Escort, Inc**
	(Control unauthorized access)	(observe & report deficiencies)	(e.g., guide, accompany, inspect, special assignment)
**RISK (Random or Non-Random; choice of person premise)	**Intent**	**Capacity**	**Opportunity**
	to take risk to do evil deed	to take risk to do evil deed	to take risk to do evil deed
**PHASES of an ATTACK (spontaneous or non-spontaneous; against person or premise)	**Invitation**	**Confrontation**	**Attack**
	-to attack	- acceptance or - rejection	-no attempt -implemented -incomplete -complete

PRIMARY: the goal: the major role of the organization is to show support for and participation in benchmark intervention; security awareness is a constant presence. An important first step in the accepted concept that "Security is everybody's business," is to educate people as to the consequences of their decision to act or not to act.

SECONDARY: the goal: to intervene before an incident. It is different from Primary in that it anticipates why employees need to follow the policy. It is different than Tertiary in the Secondary attempts to interface with people prior to actual crimes being attempted and/or perpetrated.

TERTIARY: the goal: to reduce the probability of a perpetrator attempting and/or completing a criminal act as long as the perpetrator and premises are controlled.

The Lombardi Predatory Prevention Matrix
Reprinted with permission from Lombardi Associates, Inc.

Probability Cells vs. Possibility Cells		
PHASES of ATTACK	**Random**	**Non-Random**
(foreseeability)	(no opportunity)	(opportunity exists)
Spontaneous (no time gaps in phases)	*DEFENSE* (probability)	(possibility)
Non-Spontaneous (time gaps in phases)	(possibility)	*PLAINTIFF* (probability)

Without policy, and more specifically written policy, there can be no anticipation of police deviance or negligent behavior. Consequently, security is documented only in the administrator's mind. While some departments have written policies others have patterns of practice. Patterns of practice, however, are not documented and may open up the department to claims of negligence should something go wrong. For example, exceeding the speed limit in response to emergencies is a common practice in policing. Without written documentation that stipulates how fast over the speed limit is reasonable or what emergencies warrant the excessive speed, the department or officer can be held liable for negligent actions should a person be injured or property destroyed.

In thinking about policy, the police manager must identify what the problem is and what resolution is appropriate. Drucker (1974) explained that concepts of business are not abstractions but rather action commitments through which a department will carry out its objectives. Furthermore, they provide standards for which those objectives may be measured. This may simply be utilized as a strategy for effective use of force policy. "Objectives are needed in all areas on which the survival of the business depends. The specific targets, the goals in any objective area, depend on the strategy of the individual business" (Drucker, 1974, p. 100). Taking a critical look into the objectives, goals and strategies of a law enforcement agency and putting those concepts to work, police executives foster a relationship between members of the organization. This application is also construed as an effort to establish internal security. A policy and procedure manual that governs departmental protocol is arguably the most cogent and standard means available to disseminate information and promote the organization's philosophy and mission.

Definitions. It is important to define policy and procedure, as the two are not synonymous. A *policy* is defined as "A definite course or method of action to guide and determine present and future decisions, or a guide to decision-making under a given set of circumstances within the framework of corporate objectives, goals and management philosophies" (Bizmanuals.com, 2001). A *procedure,* on the other hand, is often defined as a particular or consistent way of doing something. Furthermore, it explains how to implement or carry out a policy. Both provide accountability measures for the department. Consider, for example, use of force policies. *Graham v. Connor* (1989), which measures whether an officer's use of force is objectively reasonable in light of the facts and circumstances, is a U.S. Supreme Court case that corresponds with most departmental force policies. To deviate from this policy may criminally or civilly implicate the officer and department. Likewise, a deviation from a departmental procedure on how to effect a use of force option may be just as detrimental to the officer or department.

Communication. A policy and procedure manual serves as an explicit means of translation between the administration and the rest of the organization. Once the department's philosophies have been identified and implemented, the manual is the most effective means of communicating that information. Explicit knowledge, as conveyed in a policy manual, is easily passed on to others due to its formal and systematic processes and definitions. Certain members of the organization may implicitly know the philosophies; however, it cannot be assumed that they are known by the organization as a whole. Through a written means of communication "…this knowledge is shared and understood as an explicit body of knowledge. The purpose is to disseminate information, inform members of the organization about recent management decisions or to signal the community about organizational purpose" (Kinnaird, 2001, p. 75).

Time. Mandatory retraining is a large part of work in contemporary police society and consumes numerous hours both inside and outside of police duty. Although police academies, workshops, and seminars provide basic instruction in use of force activities, they oftentimes do not consider departmental policies and procedures. It is therefore up to individual departments to train their members on the expectations, goals and objectives of the organization in respect to use of force activities. Despite changes in personnel, administrations or laws, a policy manual will reduce training time because it serves as a functional guide that is constant and can be used as a reference. It provides know-how and instruction to not only new recruits but to those existing personnel members. This can reduce the need for training or retraining in respect to certain aspects of departmental protocol. Furthermore, many policy manuals reiterate duties as instructed at police academies, promoting an acquired knowledge in an effort to maintain standards of service. Mandatory retraining, then, can be left for the acquisition of new knowledge for other law enforcement functions.

Strengthening operations. When an organization acquires knowledge collectively they also benefit collectively. Although the mission may be the same, law enforcement agencies are made up of many different divisions and written policy in the use of force ensures that everyone in the department follows appropriate agendas. From detectives to jailers to department heads, it is critical that each member of the organization understands and interprets their positional objectives and capabilities as well as the overall departmental objective. Providing a written communication method that is comprehensive in respect to all divisions will promote quality and consistent directives that should be followed by all members of the organization.

Hicks (1967) explained that administrative and strategic planning is critical to the proper functioning of departmental operations. In developing a policy and procedure manual, police managers must provide for growth and efficiency of objectives. If an organization is to remain healthy, it must pursue realistic objectives as well. "Effective plans are flexible, and adapt to changing conditions" (Hicks, 1967, p. 253). The old adage explaining that it is much easier to keep the patient well than it is to cure his sickness is true to a certain extent. Police administrators must anticipate changes and emergencies in the organization both internally and externally. If an inmate in the county jail needs medical treatment, a determination of who will handle the transportation must be made. Will there be sufficient help in their place should something happen? Likewise, changes in case law may require a reorganization of departmental procedures. Finally, crime and societal threats are always changing with changes in population and demographics. Although there exists a principle of commitment in establishing the goals and objectives of a police organization, there is even more of a commitment in putting those objectives to work.

CONTROL

Control is the second cell of the predatory prevention matrix. Having established policy as the foundation of this four-stage model, a police organization can successfully control its assets through documentation. To defend a police agency in an excessive force lawsuit, it must be illustrated that there exists an interaction between policy and control. Essentially, was policy developed through a study of documentation? Control in this model is defined as the necessary documentation of the proposed resolution of the defined problem. This becomes a continuous and dynamic process, as policy must constantly change with the environment and be redefined. This ensures consistency, certainty, and stability in the organization. It also defines vulnerability exposure to the organization's assets. Lombardi (1996) explained that control documentation is a proactive prevention method to reduce negligence or deviance before they end up controlling those assets.

If criminal opportunity is to be reasonably determined and preventive planning to be considered, security risks must be identified through control documentation measures. Police incident reports and use of force forms tend to be the most critical benchmarks when lawsuits are imminent. Khulman (1989) explained, "Because there is no way to prove what did happen, there is no way to prove what did not happen, so you have no way to defend yourself against false accusations" (p. 356). Additionally, statistics are essential in providing police administrators with control measures. Types, frequency and circumstances of force are recorded and evaluated to determine how well the components are functioning. This determination may be based upon an individual officer or the effectiveness of the entire group as a whole, e.g., drug enforcement unit, bike patrol, SWAT, etc.

Performance evaluations are another control measure for the agency. Feedback from all sources, positive and negative, ensures equitable guidance in the officer following new goals as well as following existing ones. Measuring performance judges the overall efficiency and effectiveness of the agency. Effectiveness is defined as the *degree* of achieving goals while efficiency encompasses the manner in which goals are achieved (Anderson, 1998). Although these two concepts appear synonymous, they are not. In fact, effectiveness can be viewed as subsequent to efficiency due to the mobility and facilitation of resource management within the process of efficiency. For example, a police manager that exhibits proper skills in communication, and facilitates information-oriented programs within the department, will better provide them with appropriate tools to elicit effective public service by their own means.

Other control measures to consider would be employment background checks and employee assistance programs. Consider the law enforcement officer that has been known to use excessive force in effecting police duty. A supervisor must address this problem. Once identified, it is the administrator's responsibility, based upon the circumstances, to place that officer into an appropriate program to resolve the conflict. This may be in the form of training, retraining, orientation or anger management courses. As a result, not only has the police supervisor attempted to resolve the problem, it explicitly conveys their effort to do so.

With the independent and discretionary nature of police work, administrators are not always aware of an officer's actions. Policy and control documentation, then, signals to the organization and community that policy must be followed and deviance from it will result in reparations, rehabilitation, or termination. From a litigation standpoint, policy and control documentation impacts the foreseeability of negligent or deviant opportunity by an officer. "Reasonable or adequate security is situational and interrelated with risk factors associated with foreseeability and legal notice" (Lombardi, 1998, p. 261). The basic elements of risk comprise the third cell of the predatory prevention matrix.

RISK

In almost all civil litigation cases against the police, the organization must prove that it used its control documentation and policies to determine the risk of negligent or deviant opportunities by officers. For purposes of this model, risk is defined as the intent, capacity, and opportunity to commit such acts. "Since professional 'learned' methodology is not and should not be based on fortune-telling, we cannot know of an individual's intent without any further information" (Lombardi, 1997, p. 23). This same philosophy is apparent with capacity. Opportunity, however, is the only factor a police organization can control ahead of time. By using policy and control, opportunity can be reduced before an incident occurs. Consequently, an opportunity would never be acted upon despite the officer's intent or capacity to do so. When looking at opportunity, however, it must be understood that it cannot exist without intent and capacity. *Intent* is the desire to commit a deviant act. It is seldom proved by direct evidence, therefore it is difficult to know in advance exactly what an individual's intent is. *Capacity* is the competence to take a risk by committing the act or understanding the consequences of the act (Lombardi, 1997).

Consider police official deviance, as this is oftentimes a breeding ground for negligence due to opportunistic circumstances. Chevigny (1969) explained, "The policeman sees his job to be catching criminals, not complying with procedures" (p. 150). New transfers and rookie police officers must "unlearn" much of what is learned in the police academy or from prior service with other agencies. More than just adhering to new policy, officers must learn the unwritten rules promulgated by the organization. This often comes in the form of "playing the game" regarding the officially sanctioned deviation from formal procedures (Tifft, 1970). The legitimization of this deviance is substantiated through a common understanding of needs in police work. Chevigny (1969) explained that without official deviance, officers would be hampered and ineffective. With the collective effort of policing, is there a reciprocal responsibility of the organization to those who occupy its offices? Barker and Roebuck (1973) concluded in their investigation that the real organizational task of police administrators is not so much keeping their officers honest but managing the level of police deviance so that work may be done without arousing public outrage. Lies and deception are familiar forms of official police deviance. "Deception of civilians untutored in their legal rights makes police work simpler and gets the job done" (Lee, 1981, p. 206).

Officers may be asked by superiors to change or fabricate their incident reports in an effort to reduce ambiguity or add evidence for convictions. Consider deadly force by officers, as this is often a continuous point of contention relative to police deviance from procedure. This may or may not be independent of "officially sanctioned" deviance as previously described but still represents risk attributed to opportunity. Kohler (1975) analyzed 1500 situations of deadly force where evidence was seriously questioned regarding the need to resort to that level of force. In the study, Kohler found only three of the 1500 cases where the officer or officers were subjected to criminal punishment for their actions. Did opportunities exist for deviant or negligent police actions? Was it a result of poor policy or control documentation? The answer could be yes. However, it would be problematic in determining the premise of the deviancy, either officially sanctioned or not. The point here is that opportunities for deviant police behavior do exist and are determined by various circumstances created by the organization. Therefore, it is critical for police administrators to not only implement good policy and control it, but to make sure that they control those who supervise others.

FORESEEABILITY

Phases of attack is the fourth and final stage of the predatory prevention model. This particular cell is used to determine foreseeability and notice. Foreseeability is defined as "the reasonable anticipation or expectation that harm or injury can result from the commission or omission of certain acts" (Lombardi, 1996, p. 422). Conversely, notice is the communication of the knowledge of a fact and is usually conducted by a police supervisor. Quarles (1989) explained that any attack has particular stages: an invitation, a confrontation, and an assault.

An invitation is any situation or circumstance that prompts an initiation of a crime or deviant or negligent act. For example, a female walking alone at night in a poorly lighted area may provoke an attack from a violator. Likewise, a traffic stop arrest, or attempted arrest, that escalates into a physical force situation due to poor tactics, knowledge, supervision or lack of police assistance, also defines an invitation. Additionally, an invitation that produces officer negligence may be the result of a gap in time whereby backup officers or administrators have yet to arrive to the scene.

A confrontation to an attack is anything that deters or makes the invitation less attractive. "If the criminal does not face sufficient confrontation, because the opportunity was not reduced or removed, it is probable that he or she will commit the crime" (Lombardi, 2001, p. 63). Proper backup officers, knowledge through training, and appropriate force responses provide confrontational circumstances for the potential police resistor or attacker. Those same circumstances also serve as a "control" against an officer who attempts a deviant act against the violator himself.

An assault is the action commitment or the end result of an invitation. It is the very element that is to be prevented through proper policy and control documentation. Time, as mentioned previously, is a factor that relates to all three elements regarding the assault. This aspect regarding spontaneity also provides the premise of this cell of the matrix.

A spontaneous attack conceptualizes all three phases as having occurred simultaneously. In other words, if the phases of an attack occur within seconds, there is insufficient time to prevent a negative event from occurring. The lack of a time gap between phases provides support for the defense in litigation. Conversely, a non-spontaneous attack has differential time gaps between the invitation and confrontation phases or confrontation and assault. This time gap "represents the element of foreseeability that supports a claim of non-spontaneous or planned attack on the plaintiff" (Lombardi, 1996, p. 423). Furthermore, if there is sufficient time for appropriate intervention, the event is also not spontaneous. As a model, this is critical when considering proactive organizational planning prior to an incident or as a reactive assessment relative to damage control.

In addition to the Predatory Prevention Matrix as a social science model of proximate cause, many questions can and should be asked by officers and administrators in an effort to reduce a department's liability profile. The Gallagher-Westfall Group, Inc. provided ten specific questions that law enforcement *administrators* should ask:

- Does my department provide constant training and updates in critical legal areas?
- Do the officers in my department have ready access to competent, experienced legal advice and counsel?
- Do the officers in my department feel comfortable with their knowledge of the law, especially laws of arrest, search and seizure, and use of force?
- Does my department provide officers with frequent exposure to contextual training, scenarios and simulations focusing on these critical areas, testing their knowledge and decision-making skills?

- Do my officers constantly prepare themselves for the use of force by previewing potential situations and determining what level of force might be appropriate?
- Does my department consistently review its use of force incidences?
- When reviewing these incidences, is it required that officers incorporate all the details that could be seen to justify the level of force or the officer's perception of the seriousness of the offense and the threat?
- Do the officers in my department practice the verbal, physical, and legal skills associated with their tasks so that they are comfortable under stress and reflexively come up with the proper response?
- Do the officers in my department constantly evaluate performance as if all of it was on videotape and view how it might be replayed in court?
- Is every aspect of my department's performance in the community such that potentially hostile witnesses would be supportive of the officer's actions?

Likewise, Jeff Chudwin, President of the Illinois Tactical Officer's Association, provided questions that hold *officers* accountable for their actions through training and policy review:

- Have you received any training in constitutional limitations related to police use of force since basic training?
- If so, do you have written documentation as to the date, the length of the training, the content, and who did the instruction?
- Does your department have a written use of force policy?
- Do you possess a copy?
- When did you last review this policy?
- If called before a civil jury, can you accurately describe the policy?
- If asked about your knowledge regarding the content of the policy, what is the only acceptable answer you can give?
- What is the next logical question?
- Do you possess federal and state statutes on use of force?
- When did you last review these laws?

- If called before a jury, can you explain your understanding of constitutional and statutory limitations?
- When did you last receive less-than-lethal force training?
- Are you carrying a baton, chemical spray, stun gun, etc. without written documentation and certification of training?
- Does your agency require refresher training in use of force procedure, tactics, and physical skills?

If any of these questions are answered negatively or with serious doubts or questions, it is time to take action steps to reduce your department's liability profile!

LAWS

FEDERAL STATUTE
Regarding Use of Force

"Violation of Constitutional rights under 'color of law' "
42 U.S.C. 1983 (Civil Rights Act)

Every person who, under color of any statute, ordinance, regulation, custom, or usage of any state or territory, subjects, or causes to be subject, any citizen of the United States or other person within the jurisdiction thereof to the deprivation of any rights, privileges, or immunities secured by the Constitution and laws, shall be liable to the party injured in an action at law, suit in equity, or other proper proceeding for damages.

To succeed under a Section 1983 claim, the plaintiff must establish several points:
There was an injury to the plaintiff;
This injury involved a violation of a constitutional right or a federal law;
The defendant was a person. Also includes cities and counties when injuries occur in their jails. States and state agencies cannot be liable under Section 1983;
The defendant was acting "under color of law";
Must show deliberate indifference.

Excessive force claims, deadly or not, in <u>seizing</u> an individual fall under the "objective reasonableness" standard of the 4th Amendment.

> ***Graham v. Connor*, 109 S. Ct. 1865 (1989)**
> ***Tennessee v. Garner*, 105 S. Ct. 1 (1985)**
> ***Austin v. Hamilton*, 945 F.2d 1155 (10th Cir. 1991)**

Claims arising from **force in jails**, including *deliberate indifference* will fall under the 8th Amendment.

***Tennessee v. Garner*, 105 S. Ct. 1 (1985)**

Cases involving officers using force likely to cause death or great bodily harm to prevent an arrest from being defeated by resistance or escape.

Rule #1: When it is necessary to prevent escape AND
Rule #2: the officer has probable cause to believe that the suspect poses a significant threat of death or serious physical injury to the officer or others.
Rule #3: A warning should be given prior to using force if feasible.

***Graham v. Connor*, 109 S. Ct. 1865 (1989)**

U.S. Supreme Court decided that in all cases, regardless of the force level employed, courts and juries must examine the facts to determine the "objective reasonableness" of the force used, from the perspective of the reasonable officer.

STATE STATUTE
Regarding Use of Force

"Proximate cause of intentional or negligent harm"
(Example: Kansas Statute: K.S.A. 21-3215)

A law enforcement officer, or any person whom such officer has summoned or directed to assist in making a lawful arrest, need not retreat or desist from efforts to make a lawful arrest because of resistance or threatened resistance to the arrest. Such officer is justified in the use of any force which such officer reasonably believes to be necessary to effect the arrest and of any force which such officer reasonably believes to be necessary to defend the officer's self or another from bodily harm while making the arrest. However, such officer is justified in using force likely to cause death or great bodily harm only when such officer or another person, or when such officer reasonably believes that such force is necessary to prevent the arrest from being defeated by resistance or escape and such officer has probable cause to believe that the person to be arrested has committed, or attempted to commit, a felony involving great bodily harm or is attempting to escape by use of a deadly weapon, or otherwise indicates that such person will endanger human life, or inflict great bodily harm, unless arrested without delay.

A law enforcement officer making an arrest pursuant to an invalid warrant is justified in the use of any force which such officer would be justified in using if the warrant were valid, unless such officer knows that the warrant is invalid.

HISTORY: L. 1969, ch. 180; **21-3215**; L. 1990, ch. 98; 1; L. 1993, ch.69; 1; July 1.

(*Note: Kansas laws concerning self defense, defense of a dwelling, and defense of non-dwelling property, apply to police as well as private citizens. Review K.S.A. 21-3211, 3212, 3213 for applicable laws.*)

To succeed under a state tort, the plaintiff must establish several, general points:

1. *There existed a duty;*
2. *There existed a breach of that duty;*
3. *The breach was the proximate cause of injury.*

LEGAL CITATIONS FOR USE OF FORCE REFERENCE

U.S. Supreme Court Cases

City of Canton v. Harris: 109 S.Ct. 1197 (1989)
"police training, deliberate indifference"

Graham v. Connor: 109 S.Ct. 1865 (1989)
"whether the officer's use of force is objectively reasonable in light of the facts and circumstances"

Tennessee v. Garner: 105 S.Ct. 1694 (1985)
"restriction on use of deadly force against fleeing felons"

Federal Court Cases

Brothers v. Klevenhagen: 28 F.3d 452 (1994)
"deadly force not unconstitutional to prevent escape of subject in custody"

Elliott v. Leavitt: 99 F.3d 640 (1996)
"quantity of bullets fired does not prove excessive force"

Forrett v. Richardson: 112 F.3d 416 (1997)
"suspect need not be armed to pose threat of 'serious harm'"

O'Neal v. DeKalb County, GA: 850 F.2d 653 (1988)
"no obligation to use minimum amount of force"

Popow v. City of Margate, NJ: 476 F.Supp. 1237 (1979)
"firearms training standards"

Reed v. Cheney: 133 F.3d 916 (1998)
"reasonable officer perception is what matters in deadly force decisions"

Scott v. Henrich: 39 F.3d 912 (1994)
"issue is reasonableness, not whether other options were available"

State Court Cases

Brach v. McGeeney: 718 A.2d 631 (1998)
"kneeling on suspect to facilitate handcuffing is reasonable"

Passino v. New York: 689 N.Y.2d 258 (1999)
"use of OC was objectively reasonable under the circumstances and did not constitute excessive force"

SUMMARY

By virtue of the four stages of the Predatory Prevention Matrix, deviant opportunity can accurately be pinpointed. Likewise, it can be proved that excessive force was anticipated and planned for, regardless of the act. If control is documented properly through policy, it is unreasonable to expect police supervisors to have foreseen the possibility of negligent use of force if the incident was unpredictable. Anticipation through a proximate cause analysis of negligent incidences provides the police administrator and trainer with effective tools to protect the organization's assets. With today's litigious society, internal security is of integral importance to a police organization. The practice of effective communication through policy and control creates the opportunity to reduce liability risk by defining the problem and increasing awareness to it. Consequently, proactive planning through an understanding of organizational dynamics and common sense control measures produces safe and effective service opportunities for law enforcement. It is also critical for departments and their officers to analyze and review federal, state and administrative policy specific to the use of force. It is from these three entities that litigation is spawned and becomes detrimental to the organization and the community.

1. What is the purpose of a use of force risk assessment model in law enforcement?

2. Compare and contrast *policy, control, risk,* and *phases of attack* as elements of the Predatory Prevention Matrix.

3. Review Section 1983 of the U.S. Code. How is this applicable to law enforcement?

4. Compare and contrast *Tennessee v. Garner* and *Graham v. Connor*. What are the variables that must be discerned in each law?

5. Research and review YOUR state use of force law. Is your departmental policy in accordance with said law? Is it more restrictive?

REFERENCES

Anderson, R. E., & Carter, I. (1998*). Human Behavior in the Social Environment: A Social System Approach* (5th ed.). New York: Aldine de Gruyter.

Barker, T., & Roebuck, J. (1973). *Typology of Police Corruption.* Springfield, IL: Charles C. Thomas.

Bennett, W. J. (1994). *The Index of Leading Cultural Indicators: Facts and Figures on the State of American Society.* New York: Simon & Schuster.

Bizmanuals.com (2001). *The Complete Policies and Procedures System* [On-line]. Available: www.bizmanuals.com.

Chevigny, P. (1969). *Police Power.* New York: Pantheon.

Doyle, M. R. (1994, February). Admissions of Dishonesty. *Security Concepts, 1,* (6) 9.

Drucker, P. F. (1974). *Management: Tasks, Responsibilities, Practices.* New York: Harper and Row.

Fournies, F. F. (1987). *Coaching for Improved Work Performance.* Blue Ridge Summit, PA: Liberty Hall Press.

Graham v. Connor, 109 S. Ct. 1865 (1989).

Hicks, H. G. (1967). *The Management of Organizations: A Systems and Human Resources Approach.* New York: McGraw Hill.

Kinnaird, B. A. (Winter, 2001). Repositories of Knowledge: A Critical Look into a Knowledge System of Police Management. *The Journal, 7,* 74-79.

Kohler, A. (1975). Police Homicide in a Democracy. *Journal of Social Issues, 31,* 163-170.

Kuhlman, R. S. (1989). *Safe Places? Security Planning and Litigation*. Charlottesville, VA: Michie Company.

Lee, J. A. (1981). Official Deviance in the Legal System. *Law and Deviance*. H. L. Ross.

Lombardi, J. H. (1996). Workplace Violence: Anticipation Through Process, Not Prediction of Results. In L. J. Fennelly (ed.), *the Handbook of Loss Prevention and Crime Prevention* (pp. 414-426). Butterworth Publishers.

Lombardi, J. H. (1997, December). Randomness and Spontaneity in Security Negligence Premises Litigation. *Security Journal, 9,* 23-27.

Lombardi, J. H. (1998). Accurate Use of Criminological Theory vs. Legal Misconception of Best Practices: $4.5 Million Jury Verdict. *Security Journal, 11,* (2-3), 259-264.

Lombardi, J. H. (2001, May). Not Guilty by Reason of Security. *Security Management*, 62-69.

Quarles, C. L. (1989). School Violence: a Survival Guide for School Staff. National Education Association. Washington, DC.

Tifft, T. (1970). *Comparative Police Supervision Systems and Organizational Analysis*. Unpublished Doctoral Dissertation, University of Illinois.

Chapter 3 – Use of Force Policy

Conveying a management philosophy through a policy manual would be less difficult if police administrations shared similar philosophies. This, however, is not the case in many instances due to the ever-changing structures of police organizations. Raine (1999) explained that the problems that many agencies face is due to working together both internally and externally. There are often conflicting objectives and priorities for the department despite the common goal of public service. For example, county law enforcement agencies, unlike their municipal counterparts, hold elections where the propensity for new administrations every four years is quite realistic. Philosophies and goals on how to effectively provide public service using appropriate tools and resources may be different from previous administrations. On the other hand, municipal agencies may employ a department head for numerous years with philosophies and goals becoming complacent in nature. Additionally, it is not uncommon for two departments existing in the same jurisdiction to have separate goals and means to achieving those goals. The changing structure of police organizations, or the lack thereof, and the reality of working with other departments, or facets of the criminal justice system, produces conflict for police administrators who wish to develop policies and procedures. Unfortunately, our complex society does not function with a compatible set of values to serve as its basis. "Individuals working in the various components of the system, personnel in various jurisdictions, and influence bearers who have an interest in the administration of justice, are extremely unlikely to agree on a single set of values" (Wright, 1999, p. 41).

From a departmental perspective, police managers may face difficulties in producing or revising use of force policies and procedures because of obscure divisional objectives. Skoler (1977) and Kellogg (1976) described a monolithic system of justice administration characterized by its structural analyses in organizations. The divisions, for instance, which make up a police agency, may not function as a true system. A lack of coherence and unity is exhibited, leaving the police organization in further dismay when trying to build on positive objectives within the department itself. If a detective division cannot provide clear goals and methods of operation for its own cause, and adhere to those standards, it will not be able to contribute to the overall objectives of the organization. Unfortunately, many police agencies produce internal divisions and expect them to organize themselves. It is better to lay a definitive foundation of policies and expectations for the department first and allow subsequent divisions to utilize those goals and procedures as prerequisites to their own operation. Additional areas have also shown to produce problems in the creation or revision of use of force policies and procedures.

Funds. Weisheit (1999) explained that funds are limited in respect to staffing and special functions within the organization. Departments that function on limited budgets and without help from grants or other facets of financial resolve, will provide personnel, equipment and use of force training as the budget allows. If police organizations attempt to meet the changing needs of the community as well as strive to satisfy their own needs, the effort must be outlined by new operational objectives. Funding to provide the organization the means to pursue these objectives is critical. Without it, the department's policies will remain with little chance at revision or construction.

Message breakdown. However communication may be delivered in the organization, vagueness is all too common. Existing manuals may contain poorly chosen words and phrases, poor organization of ideas, awkward sentence structure and a failure to clarify implications.

Psychological barriers. "We often have preconceived ideas as to what people 'really' mean; when we hear something new we tend to identify it with something similar that we have experienced in the past" (Federal Bureau of Investigation, 1999, pp. 26-27). It is difficult to ensure proper construction and implementation of use of force policy when there is conflict with personnel. Stereotyping may occur as the result of police managers letting expectations determine meaning in communication. This particular reason is why so many police agencies leave out certain areas and members of the organization in assisting with new policies and procedures.

Perception. Much like a traffic accident whereby many parties will give a different account, all members of an organization see things differently. Even though they are working for a common objective, this can be a source of significant conflict for the police manager. Effective supervisors must understand that they need reliance on subordinates for information. Internal communication must be upward, downward and horizontal. Through most agency directives, however, these tasks are formally transmitted downward. No guide has been developed in *what* information a subordinate must communicate upward.

Written communications. Simply stated, clear writing begins with clear thinking. Contemporary police society is inundated with lawsuits and liability factors. Subsequently, there is a tendency to document every act, decision and statement that is made. Unfortunately, policy manuals become obscure due to the repetitive information regarding how to avoid particular legal situations. Use of force policies may be implemented by simply clarifying the objective through thoughtful analysis.

Listening. Listening is not a passive process. This seemingly easy task is the culprit of more miscommunication and conflict than necessary. Unfortunately the key players in organizing use of force policy and procedure, e.g., administration, subordinates, community, tend to listen to only what they want to hear. An idea or thought in how to appropriate funds towards use of force training, or to outline certain objectives, may go unheard by an individual who is threatened by that potential task.

Standards. What constitutes a policy? Barker (1994) expressed that standards cannot cover every possible aspect of work requirements. Because of this phenomenon, there exist written and unwritten rules. Even though police administrators recognize that full enforcement is impossible, the public entity is in constant demand for answers to everything. Discretion and "unwritten rules" become the substitute where discrete policies cannot be enacted. Writing speeding tickets for only ten miles over the speed limit, disposing of alcoholic containers possessed by juveniles after midnight, not arresting prostitutes but instead having them "move on" are just some examples. Another conflict that shadows this process is that whether or not a rule is written, there are ramifications that may include criminal or civil liability.

Figures 3.1-3.9 denote policy implications involving departments' use of force in 1996-1998 as researched and recorded by the International Association of Chiefs of Police. This serves as an explicit illustration of the improvements made in policy and control documentation that assists in risk assessment and management of the use of force function in criminal justice service. Furthermore, a sample of a use of force policy can be viewed in (Appendix A) and used as a model for "best practices" in policy creation and implementation.

POLICY AND PROCEDURE MODEL

Many different names have encompassed the explicit communication of policies and procedures. "Standard Operating Procedures" (SOP), "Department Operating Procedures" (DOP) and "Quality Operating Procedures" (QOP) are just a few. Despite the name, it is critical to understand that these are general, written documents that support and guide departmental policies. Providing definitions of use of force policy and procedure and how the police administration wishes to implement those procedures is paramount to a successful and complete policy guide.

Figure 3.1
DEPARTMENT HAS A FORMAL USE OF FORCE POLICY

1996-1998

Year	Yes (count)	No (count)	Totals	Yes (percent)	No (percent)
1996	26	0	26	100	0
1997	52	0	52	100	0
1998	30	0	30	100	0

Figure 3.2
DEPARTMENT HAS A FORMAL DISCIPLINARY POLICY

1996-1998

Year	Yes (count)	No (count)	Totals	Yes (percent)	No (percent)
1996	25	2	27	92.6	7.4
1997	47	5	52	90.4	9.6
1998	30	0	30	100.0	0.0

Figure 3.3

DEPARTMENT HAS A POLICY ON THE
USE OF FORCE CONTINUUM

1996-1998

Year	Yes (count)	No (count)	Totals	Yes (percent)	No (percent)
1996	26	1	27	96.3	3.7
1997	52	0	52	100.0	0.0
1998	29	1	30	97.0	3.0

Figure 3.4
DEPARTMENT HAS A FORMAL
USE OF FORCE CONTINUUM

1996-1998

Year	Yes (count)	No (count)	Totals	Yes (percent)	No (percent)
1996	24	3	27	88.9	11.1
1997	51	1	52	98.1	1.9
1998	29	1	30	97.0	3.0

Figure 3.5
DEPARTMENT REQUIRES A WRITTEN REPORT
ON ALL USE OF FORCE INCIDENTS

1996-1998

Year	Yes (count)	No (count)	Totals	Yes (percent)	No (percent)
1996	26	1	27	96.3	3.7
1997	50	2	52	96.2	3.8
1998	30	0	30	100.0	0.0

Figure 3.6
DEPARTMENT HAS AUTOMATED DATABASE FOR
TRACKING USE OF FORCE INCIDENTS

1996-1998

Year	Yes (count)	No (count)	Totals	Yes (percent)	No (percent)
1996	21	6	27	77.8	22.2
1997	38	14	52	73.1	26.9
1998	21	9	30	70.0	30.0

Figure 3.7
DEPARTMENT HAS A FORMAL REVIEW PROCESS
FOR USE OF FORCE INCIDENTS

1996-1998

Year	Yes (count)	No (count)	Totals	Yes (percent)	No (percent)
1996	23	4	27	85.2	14.8
1997	45	7	52	86.5	13.5
1998	30	0	30	100.0	0.0

Figure 3.8
ALL USE OF FORCE COMPLAINTS ROUTINELY
INVESTIGATED BY DEPARTMENT

1996-1998

Year	Yes (count)	No (count)	Totals	Yes (percent)	No (percent)
1996	25	2	27	92.6	7.4
1997	47	5	52	90.4	9.6
1998	28	2	30	93.3	6.7

Figure 3.9
DEPARTMENT HAS A POLICY ON THE
USE OF FORCE CONTINUUM

1996-1998

Year	Yes (count)	No (count)	Totals	Yes (percent)	No (percent)
1996	17	10	27	63	37
1997	36	16	52	69	31
1998	26	4	30	87	13

Many criminal justice agencies have use of force policy and procedure. The style, length and composition are different among agencies but congruent with the agency's goals and objectives as well as the community's needs. Considering this, use of force policy should be revised and updated continually to meet those needs. Whether a new policy is in effect or an existing policy is modified, it must be documented and distributed accordingly so that all members are aware and can take immediate action. Page (1998) and Bizmanuals.com (2001) provide insight into the organization of policy and procedure components. "An organizational structure provides the framework within which decisions are made" (Page, 1998, p. 5).

Organization

How many current use of force policies are read? How many of them are continually used as a reference or a guide? If the answers to these questions are in the negative, how does one go about making a written guide useful? In developing or revising use of force policy, it is important to establish needs from the start. How it will be set up, how to add supplemental material, and just what policies and procedures will be covered, are just a few of those needs (Bizmanuals.com, 2001). Page (1998) outlines a basic format for a complete and thorough organization of a new manual, policies, or changes in an existing system that administrators can apply to use of force policy in their own agencies.

Manual type. The type of manual used in a police organization dictates how policies will be explicitly conveyed and ultimately depends upon the size of the department as well as their financial allowances. Smaller departments may benefit from one manual that conveys the missions, philosophies and duties of the organization. By contrast, a larger department may need more than one manual to express philosophies and goals for specific divisions and personnel, e.g., jail, detective, special operations. A manual grouped by departments or functional areas allows for new or revised policies to fall under a supervisor and ensures a consistent approach to policies and procedures within areas (Bizmanuals.com, 2001). It may be best, however, to provide the organization with at least one manual to envelop the goals as it relates to use of force functions of the entire agency.

Goals and objectives. Visions, objectives, and goals should be the focus of use of force policy and procedure and be displayed on the first page. The mission statement is the philosophy of the department head that runs the organization. This explicitly conveys the importance of the policy and determines the theme.

Writing format. The writing format is the structure of the policy and procedure. It will determine how the policy is organized and attempts to achieve continuity through an ease of transition between specific areas or components. It is easy for a reader to become confused when there is ambiguity in thoughts or ideas that are presented. Headings, denoted by "sections", most often serve to alleviate this problem (Page, 1998). For example, readily apparent sections in use of force policies are purpose, definitions, training, and responsibilities within administrative and legal guidelines.

Another format area of use of force policy and procedure are *optional areas.* This section relates to specific areas not covered by general policy and procedure statements and generally serves as an information source for the employee. Charts, continuums, and force report forms denote such optional areas and provide the officer with an understanding of what forms are required for specific police services. Consider also the protocol of setting up road spike systems in a vehicle pursuit. This function can be explicitly conveyed in a diagram and placed into the optional area of the policy manual. With contemporary technology, most forms and written paperwork in policing are now completed on computer database systems. If this is the case, a printed copy of the form may be added to the manual. In this sense, the optional area section provides one cohesive source for members to become knowledgeable of the structure and forms for use of force operations.

Writing style. "For communication to be effective, writers need empathy, or the ability to place themselves in the shoes of the readers and understand how the readers will view the writing" (Page, 1998, p. 59). English usage, spelling, vocabulary and grammar are just a few rules that are prerequisites to effective use of force policy. As mentioned before, organization of thoughts is also imperative, expressing logic in a process that is easy to read from sentence to sentence and paragraph to paragraph. The organization of headings and sections as described in the writing format is best used to provide clarity and easy transition. With the advent of equal opportunity laws and political correctness, gender words become problematic for the writer of a policy. Writers have used "him" historically; however, it produces a masculine bias that should be avoided when compiling the manual. Using "he" or "she" is too lengthy and awkward in conversation. It is best to use "they" or refer to the title of the specific member, e.g., deputy, officer, sergeant, lieutenant, etc. Use of force policies and procedures should be written using the most appropriate styles as needed for the department and should be impersonal and never arouse emotions in the reader. Dobbert (2001) expressed that the policy must not only be understandable between personnel but is also available to the courts, media and public in a litigation alleging "impropriety by the department." Therefore, a considerable amount of time should be dedicated to the proper organization of the use of force policy and procedure.

USE OF FORCE CONTINUUMS

Since 1984, numerous force continuums have emerged to guide decision-making when police use force. While many different scales exist, they generally serve as policy initiatives and control documentation for law enforcement agencies. This, in turn, serves as a baseline for legal and ethical actions by officers while engaged in police duty. Codified by categories that depict levels of force, these models suggest that officers have options for using force and that the officer can articulate a pragmatic response. The force levels employed by law enforcement within the scope of their powers include officer presence, verbal direction, soft and hard empty-hand control such as come-alongs and pressure-point control techniques, chemical sprays, defensive tactics, impact weapons, less-than-lethal, and finally, deadly force.

The earliest use of force continuum was developed in 1984 by Special Agent John Desmedt, who served with the U.S. Secret Service Training Division (Stetser, 2001). Called the "use of force paradigm for law enforcement," Desmedt provided that little to no recommendations existed governing the degree to which officers could use force. Consequently, he created a linear graph that depicted the officers' force actions on an *x-axis* and violator actions on a *y-axis*. Levels of force illustrated in this paradigm included officer presence, verbal stabilization, weaponless control, chemical agents, impact weapons and deadly force. The *y-axis* provided that violator actions ranged from cooperative to aggressively offensive with the propensity to cause death to the officer or others. Both axes proceeded in six stages.

Conner (1986) provided a use of force continuum shaped like a semicircle, shaded from light to dark red. Officer control was depicted through fifteen force levels from body language to the use of service weapons. Perhaps the most significant use of force continuum used today is the widely accepted Federal Law Enforcement Training Center (FLETC) model developed by Graves and Connor (1992). It depicts dual staircases with five stages, all leading to a common landing at the top (see figure 3.10). Using levels of force congruent with other scales, the continuum articulates a "reasonable officer's perception" in accordance with a violator's action. Arrows lead both up and down the steps hastening the idea that force is an escalation and de-escalation process. Indeed, force is a dynamic situation. Officers are constantly moving back and forth between control and self-defense. On one end, the officer must be able to control without being excessive in his use of force. On the other end, they must be able to protect themselves or others from force likely to cause death or great bodily harm. For example, an officer who is placed into imminent danger by an assailant with a gun is justified to use deadly force. However, if that officer subdues the assailant by a method other than deadly force, then the shift is back towards the control end of the spectrum. This difficult juxtaposition poses significant implications for legal and ethical justification of police force.

Several other use of force continuums have been created that serve as comprehensive and useful guidelines for determining levels of force. Calibre Press, Inc. provided a use of force continuum similar to the federal model in that it depicts commensurate force responses with suspect demeanor; however, this model stresses weapons and tools that are appropriate within each stage (see figure 3.11). The Illinois Law Enforcement Training and Standards Board assembled a use-of-force guideline that serves as a linear matrix discerning subject demeanor, use of force measures and potential injuries to both officer and subject in effecting force options (see figure 3.12). Another use of force model provides a "common sense" approach to using force options based upon the totality of the circumstances (see figure 3.13). Developed by Larry Lein of Law Enforcement and Security Trainers, Inc., this model provides a left-to-right articulation of force options based upon contact with a subject, decision processes gathered from common sense factors of the situation, and subsequent force options that lead to the ultimate goal of control or self-defense.

In applying levels of force that are reasonable, officers do not have to move through all levels of the continuum. Furthermore, it is not necessary for them to proceed through the continuum in a sequential manner. An officer who makes a routine traffic stop and is suddenly faced with a driver who immediately exits his vehicle and points a gun at him, is not going to first use passive contact control measures, chemical sprays, impact weapons, and then his firearm before taking action. Unfortunately, many policies in law enforcement agencies depict such chaos in articulating use of force protocol. To complicate matters further, many agencies do not provide their officers with various force options such as chemical agents, impact weapons or less-than-lethal weapons. When options are eliminated, officers are then forced to move up to the next level of force, which may or may not be legally and ethically appropriate for the situation.

Reasonable officer's perception	Enforcement electives	Reasonable officer's response
Assaultive (Serious bodily harm/death)	V	Deadly force
Assaultive (bodily harm)	IV	Defensive tactics
Resistant (Active)	III	Compliance techniques
Resistant (passive)	II	Contact control
Compliant (cooperative)	I	Verbal commands

Source: Franklin Graves and Gregory Connor,
The Federal Law Enforcement Training Center, Glynco, Georgia

Figure 3.10 Federal Law Enforcement Training Center's Use-of-Force Model

70

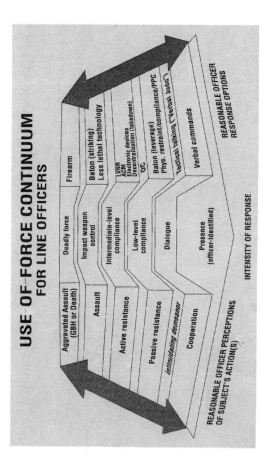

Figure 3.11 Use-of-Force Continuum for Line Officers

GBH   Great Bodily Harm   OC   Oleoresin Capsicum
ACM   Active Counter-measures   PPC   Pressure Point Control
LVNR   Lateral Vascular Neck Restraint (Lindell System)

Reprinted with permission from Calibre Press, Inc.

Figure 3.12 Use of force Guidelines Drafted by the Illinois Law Enforcement Training and Standards Board

Subject Demeanor	Potential Injury to Officer	Appropriate Control Tactics/Officer's Response	Potential Injury to Subject
Cooperation (Subject complies with verbal or other direction.	Little or none, if subject remains cooperative	Presence Verbal control Restraint devices	Abrasions/scratches Minor bruising
Passive resistance (Subject fails to respond to verbal or other direction but exhibits no resistant movement.)	Muscular/joint/ligament injury Abrasions/scratches (Injuries caused primarily by passive resister having to be lifted or removed by officer.)	Joint manipulations Pressure-sensitive area techniques Other appropriate compliance	Muscular/joint/ligament injury Abrasions/scratches Remove chance of soft tissue damage
Active resistance (Subject exhibits resistive movement to avoid physical control.)	Muscular/joint/ligament injury Abrasions/scratches Lacerations (Likelihood of injury is greatly increased, due to the dynamic movement involved.)	Stunning techniques (with or without control instruments) Takedowns Chemical agents Control instrument techniques K-9 deployment	Muscular/joint/ligament injury Abrasions/scratches Lacerations Effects of chemical agents
Aggressive assault (Subject performs physical actions, without weapons, that are aggressive and likely to cause physical injury.)	Lacerations Minor broken bones Chipped teeth Connective tissue damage Bruising (Injury potential very likely, due to subject's proximity to officer and highly agitated or combative state. Injury could result from striking or wrestling with officer.)	Punches, kicks, other striking techniques Impact tools Takedown directed at skeletal structure of body Non-lethal weapons	Lacerations Minor broken bones Chipped teeth Connective tissue damage Bruising
Deadly force (Subject takes action that will probably cause death or great bodily harm.)	Death Great bodily harm, including major broken bones, large gaping wounds, loss of organs (Likelihood of most severe injuries of all resistance categories.)	Firearms Other measures which could result in death or great bodily harm.	Death Great bodily harm, including major broken bones, large gaping wounds, loss of organs

Figure 3.13   Common Sense Use of Force Model

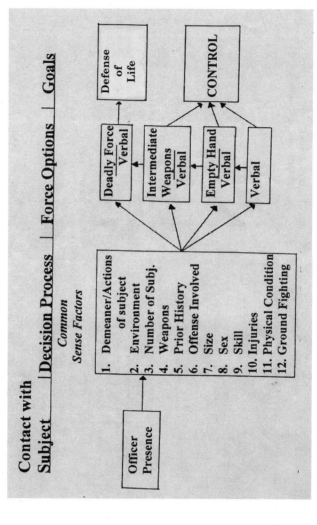

Contact with Subject | **Decision Process** | **Force Options** | **Goals**

Common Sense Factors

Officer Presence

1. Demeaner/Actions of subject
2. Environment
3. Number of Subj.
4. Weapons
5. Prior History
6. Offense Involved
7. Size
8. Sex
9. Skill
10. Injuries
11. Physical Condition
12. Ground Fighting

Deadly Force / Verbal

Intermediate Weapons / Verbal

Empty Hand / Verbal

Verbal

Defense of Life

CONTROL

Figure 3.14

List all non-striking tactics taught at your agency.

• Use a scale of 1 to 5 (1 being low and 5 being high), when comparing or evaluating techniques

Name of Technique	Level of Difficulty	Fine	Complex	Similarity	Annual Training Time per Technique
Wrist lock	4	3	4	1	30 min.

Figure 3.15 Subject Resistance Form

	TIME	LOCATION OF OCCURRENCE		DR		RD

SUSPECT'S NAME			BOOKING NO.		CHARGE	

SEX	DESCENT	HEIGHT	WEIGHT	DOB	AGE	CONNECTING REPORTS

SOURCE OF ACTIVITY
__ OBSERVED __ RADIO CALL __ CITIZEN CALL __ STATION CALL __ OTHER

CONDITIONS (CHECK ALL THAT APPLY)

__ PCP	__ MENTAL	__ FOOT PURSUIT	__ FAMILY DISPUTE	__ ASSAULT ON OFFICER
__ OTHER DRUG	__ DUI	__ OTHER TRAF. VIOL.	__ BUSINESS DISPUTE	__ ASSAULT ON CITIZEN
__ ALCOHOL	__VEH. PURSUIT	__ AIG	__ NEIGHBOR DISPUTE	__ OTHER _____

TYPE OF FORCE (CHECK ALL THAT APPLY)

PHYSICAL FORCE	CHEMICAL SPRAY	TASER VIEW FROM
BATON/SAP PAIN COMPLIANCE		TASER SERIAL NO. ____ __ FRONT __ BACK
__STRAIGHT __ TWIST LOCK	NO. TIMES SPRAYED _____	SHOW DART
__MONADNOCK __ WRIST LOCK	TYPE SPRAY USED _____	NO. OF CASETTES FIRED __ CONTACT(1,2,3)
__KUBATON __ OTHER (SPECIFY)		
__SAP _____	(MODEL NO.)_____ (EXPIR. DATE)_____	DISTANCE TO SUSPECT
		1._____
(MOTION USED) UPPER BODY	DISTANCE FROM SUSPECT	2._____
		3._____
__ STRIKE __ CAROTID	1. __ FT. 2. __ FT. 3. __ FT	
__ BLOCK __ MODIFIED CAROTID		DID DARTS PENETRATE
__ CONTROL __ LOCKED CAROTID	DURATION OF SPRAY	SKIN? __ YES __ NO
OTHER	1. __ SECS. 2. __	WAITING TIME FOR TASER
	SECS.	TO
__ KICKS	3. __	ARIVE_____
__ PUNCH	SECS.	MINUTES
__ MARTIAL ART TECHNIQUE		
__ MISCELLANEOUS PHYSICAL FORCE	WAS SPRAY EFFECTIVE:	WAS IT EFFECTIVE?
__ OTHER (SPECIFY)	__ YES __ NO	__ YES __ NO
	IF NO, REASON	
	(STATE UNK.)	IF NO, REASON
		(STATE IF UNK.)
	SHADE AREA(S) SPRAYED	

ENTER THE ONE LAST TYPE OF FORCE THAT FINALLY CONTROLLED THE SUSPECT.

EFFECTS (Check all that apply)

TIME REQUIRED TO

WAS SUSPECT INCAPACITATED? YES ____ NO ____ INCAPACITATE SUSPECT: _____ SECONDS

____ NONE APPARENT ____ CHOKING ____ FELL TO GROUND ____ CONT. SOME RESISTANCE ____ STOPPED RESISTANCE
____ EYE CLOSURE ____ COUGHING ____ ATTACKED OFCR. ____ INCREASED RESISTANCE ____ OTHER: _____

RESIDUAL EFFECTS ON OFFICERS: ____ NONE ____ CHEMICAL ____ ELECTRIC SHOCK

INJURIES RESULTING FROM TYPES: A – MAJOR (USUALLY HOSPITALIZED) B – VISIBLE (NOT HOSPITALIZED) C – COMPLAINED OIF ONLY N – NONE

	LAST NAME	TYPE INJURY	BRIEF DESCRIPTION OF INJURY	HOSPITALIZED		OFFICIO		LIGHT DUTY	
				YES	NO	YES	NO	YES	NO
OFCR.									
OFCR.									
SUSP.									

ADDITIONAL (USE OF OTHER DEVICE: I.E., FIELD TEST, ADDITIONAL OFFICER INJURED; SUSP. INJURIES UNRELATED TO USE OF FORCE; ANY OTHER PERTINENT INFO.)

USE CONTINUATION SHEET IF NECESSARY.

INVOLVED OFFICERS	SERIAL NO.	SEX	DESCENT	DIVISION/DETAIL	ON DUTY? YES ☐ ☐ NO	IN UNIFORM YES ☐ ☐ NO
					YES ☐ ☐ NO	YES ☐ ☐ NO

DATE AND TIME REPRODUCED	DIVISION	CLERK	INVESTIGATING SUPERVISOR	SERIAL NO.	DIV. DETAIL	W.C IR C.C AOORIVUBG SERIAL NO.

USE OF FORCE MANAGEMENT

The task of use of force administration is not an easy one. Considering all of the possible issues and problems that managers are inundated with on a daily basis, who has time to think about *one* particular area of policing or criminal justice authority? Shouldn't it be enough that policies exist as an explicit display of right and wrong? Can't everything work out on its own without looking over shoulders? While this may sound all too familiar for many administrators, officers, or trainers, perhaps leadership and organization that leads to effective use of force management can be decided through *systems thinking*. Not only can this philosophy satisfy use of force objectives but it can also be applied to *all* criminal justice operations within an organization.

Systems thinking can only be understood by contemplating the whole and not just the individual parts. In doing this, a law enforcement administrator must take a look at the entire organization. What it is, how it came to exist and how it can be changed for efficiency and effectiveness. In studying this phenomenon, interesting dynamics are realized. At an early age in life we are taught to break apart problems, making complex tasks more manageable. Years of this learning socialization, however, create a problem in discerning the consequences of our actions. In essence, we lose perspective regarding the larger whole! To use an old management adage, one must take a step back and see the forest for the trees.

Use of force is a complex phenomenon that must be dealt with in broad parameters through systems thinking before one can narrow the scope. This is achieved through such elements as a change in philosophy, through policy, and through training. Consider that when placed into the same system, people, however different, tend to produce similar results. The string of officers, who consistently use abusive language, have poor interpersonal communication with the public, or other members of their profession, or who use excessive force. Administrators and trainers must view underlying structures that shape individual actions.

Ultimately, it is these structures that create conditions that breed negligence or deviant behavior.

Poor use of force management, as a result of organizational dysfunction, is not new. Consider, for example, the "Parable of the Boiled Frog." Place a frog into a pan of lukewarm water on the stove and leave it undisturbed. Slowly turn up the heat and the frog will do nothing. Continue to heat the water to boiling and the frog will become groggier and groggier to the point where, although unrestricted by any means, can no longer jump out of the water to save itself. Consider also that many of today's problems come from yesterday's solutions. To rid one air bubble from a surface will only displace the bubble to another location, never truly eliminating the problem. In other words, solutions often shift problems from one part of the system to another.

Managing use of force requires a critical look at cause and effect; cause illustrating the problem and effect the problem indicator. While cause and effect are *not* closely related in time and space, administrators and trainers tend to look at the world as if they are. For example, if there is a problem in manufacturing it must be from a problem in the manufacturing line. If a salesman is not meeting his target, then there must be a problem with the salesman. The concept of systems thinking is to view the parts and the whole as separate entities and to take responsibility through accountability. Climbing the ladder of success in use of force management requires enrollment, commitment, and teamwork!

Summary

As we move further into the 21ˢᵗ century, law enforcement continues to make strides in becoming a true profession. In doing so, police administrators are expected to establish effective protocol in respect to use of force practices. The policy and procedure manual, as a systems thinking initiative, plays a strategic role in producing an environment where officers make decisions in the use of force. Furthermore, a vision and mission become working practices when promoted by this means. Police management is the fulcrum that sustains the law enforcement society and is looked upon to set the tone for the agency's goals. By a written display of knowledge through laws, training, and experience, the management team may use policy as a communication tool to serve the public in the most effective and efficient means available. As an element of police management and policy implementation, a use of force continuum serves as an explicit foundation for decision-making in use of force incidences. Although numerous continuums currently exist, it primarily serves as reciprocal direction in respect to officer and offender circumstances when attempting to control or defend.

QUESTIONS FOR DISCUSSION

1. What is *systems thinking* and how does it contribute to effective police management regarding the use of force by criminal justice practitioners?

2. Discuss the importance of use of force policy in a criminal justice agency.

3. List and describe several of the problems associated with policy creation and/or implementation. How does this affect officer performance in respect to the use of police force?

4. What purpose does a use of force continuum serve?

5. Draw and describe at least two (2) use of force continuums listed in Chapter 3. Compare and contrast the similarities and differences in the models.

REFERENCES

Barker, T. & Carter, D.L. (Eds.). (1994b). *Police Deviance* (3rd ed.). Cincinnati: Anderson.

Bizmanuals.com. (2001). *The Complete Policies and Procedures System* [On-line]. Available: www.bizmanuals.com

Connor, G. (May, 1986). Use of Force Paradigm Continuum. *Law and Order, 60,* pp. 18-19.

Dobbert, D. DlDobbert@fgcu.edu (2001, April 2). Email Interview [Personal email]. (2001, April 3).

Federal Bureau of Investigation Management Science Training Division. (1999). *Elements of Supervision.* [Training Manual]. Quantico, VA: Author.

Graves, F. R., & Connor, G. (February, 1992). The FLETC Use of Force Model. *The Police Chief,* 56-58.

Kellogg, F.R. (1976). Organizing the Criminal Justice System: A Look at Operative Objectives. *Feudal Probation, 40,* 50-56.

Page, S.B. (1998). *Establishing a System of Policies and Procedures.* Mansfield, OH: Bookmasters, Inc.

Raine, J.W. & Willson, M.J. (1999). New Public Management and Criminal Justice. In S. Stojkovic, J. Klofas & D. Kalinich (3ed.), *The Administration and Management of Criminal Justice Organizations* (pp. 239-250). Prospect Heights, IL: Waveland Press.

Skoler, D.L. (1977). *Organizing the Non-system.* Lexington, MA: Lexington Books.

Stetser, M. (2001). *The Use of Force in Police Control of Violence.* New York: LFB Scholarly Publishing.

Weisheit, R.A., Falcone, D.N. & Wells, L.E. (1999*). Crime and Policing in Rural and Small-town America.* Prospect Heights, IL: Waveland Press.

Wright, K.N. (1999). The Desirability of Goal Conflict Within the Criminal Justice System. In S. Stojkovic, J. Klofas & D. Kalinich (3ed.), *The Administration and Management of Criminal Justice Organizations* (pp. 37-49). Prospect Heights, IL: Waveland Press.

Chapter 4 – Training

As with all initiatives and issues addressed in this book, scenario or "stress"-based training has become a necessitated response in respect to litigation. Based upon Zuchel v. City of Denver (997 F.2d. 730), departments are mandated to train their officers under realistic conditions. As a contemporary style, scenario-based training serves several purposes. First, it sets precedence as to how you want your personnel to act. It also determines what skills are not being met through ordinary, static training methods. Last, a determination can be made as to how each tactic or skill can be integrated with those already established through prior training.

In contemplating these variables, significant consideration must be given to training programs as they currently exist. For example, many defensive tactics programs are clustered with techniques that may never be used in an actual conflict. Subsequently, it becomes virtually impossible to review all techniques and to validate students' abilities. In addition to the qualitative outcome measurements, a laundry list of techniques frustrates officer-trainees. They don't want to learn new things, they feel they won't remember most of them or will not need them and they don't want to be there anyway. This, unfortunately, is just a fact of life in training administration. Therefore, training programs must be scaled-down by design in order to produce a coherent set of principles with an application-based environment for optimal learning. If your defensive tactics curricula currently encompass thirty-five techniques, why not sit down with administrators and trainers and choose six techniques that are most often used in the line of duty and train with them accordingly? With just a few defensive tactics techniques in use, trainers can break down specific skills relative to those tasks and enhance learning, efficiency, and effectiveness on those tasks. It would be easy to train students in "officer down" drills in one day; however, this negates the purpose of training and fails to help officers think under stress.

Through a breakdown of skills under stress, trainers can reinforce similarities of skills they know from other tasks and can highlight conflicts with other skills that may cause a problem during a task.

Focused development through scenario-based training helps students streamline motions. The trainer can then insist on consistent repetitions of motions eventually pushing faster times, with the same outcomes. Through focused development, the trainer can also slow down the tasks to reinforce muscle memory, correct problems, or re-engage the step-by-step process. For example, the CLAMP™ program encompasses one bent-armlock technique that can be applied over twenty different ways in considering the officer's environment. While it may not be feasible to teach twenty-five applications of the CLAMP™ in a training session, focused, scenario-based curricula will assist the student in learning the foundations of the technique through breakdowns and repetition. Made up of the approach, transition, and control phases, the trainer can spend as much time as needed on the CLAMP™ technique, perfecting basic skills as applied to real-life situations. Establishing a basic grip on the violator's wrist, bending the arm back behind the center line of body, and stepping forward into the violator are all elements of one aspect of a larger system. In developing a streamlined motion with control and defensive tactics techniques, repetition through basic application best serves the student in learning and retention of the skill.

To reiterate, stress-based training provides skill acquisition as they relate to their use. From this, the trainer can program a response from the student when faced with a similar problem. Recent research suggests congruencies between heart rate and physiological responses during training exercises. Considering this, trainers can accommodate students to stressful environments accordingly in an effort to produce favorable outcomes. The San Bernardino County (CA) Sheriff's Office monitored the heart rates of trainees in the classroom after lecture and determined an average of 73 beats per minute after 1800 readings. After completing tactical responses in a scenario-based situation outside of the classroom, heart rates averaged 156 beats per minute. This difference is significant, as fine motor skills begin to deteriorate at 115 beats per minute and at 145 beats per minute complex (gross) motor skills deteriorate. As the heart beats faster, the loss of auditory and visual capabilities are imminent, leading to complete physical and cognitive dysfunction.

With stress-based training, the trainer can set up a controlled and safe environment for carrying out the training initiative. Although not "real-life", the stress simulation is enough for the student to develop a learned response to a stressful incident. Under the pressures of fear, confusion, and hyper-stimulation, your brain will seek out the first, not the best solution to the problem it's faced with. Any tactic that has an emotional attachment to it has more of a chance to be used than one drilled in a *static* environment. Without stress, these emotions take over, bringing along the tactics associated with them. When is the last time your student-trainees practiced a magazine change under stress? Or practiced handcuffing following heavy, physical activity with sweaty wrists and arms and uncooperative role-playing violators? A critical examination into scenario "stressed"-based training as a contemporary and alternative means of acquired learning may provide some insight into a necessary change for law enforcement training.

The issue of training is not one without speculation, discontent, and frustration. In fact, training is a problem for many criminal justice agencies in America, especially smaller ones. But it doesn't have to be. Before discussing the historical aspects, purpose, goals and types of training, several aspects must be recognized as contributing to the lack of training or the lack of *quality* training. For instance, the direct financial burdens for the criminal justice administrator must be taken into consideration. Instructor salaries, overtime, equipment (vehicles) and hotel expenditures must be accounted for and balanced within the scope of budgets and the ability to send officers for training. Secondly, the administrator must be concerned with manpower. Can shifts be covered? Are reserve or part-time officers and personnel available so that full-time officers may attend training? Third, what are the financial benefits of the training to the department, both directly and indirectly? Can it produce lower liability premiums and reduce medical costs? Will it decrease accidents, increase productivity and ultimately reduce the department's liability profile? Fourth, will the training have long-term implications for the agency? Will it provide needed skills acquisition for everyone? Will it increase morale and provide safer alternatives for officers? Last, will the training improve public relations? Will it protect them while preventing injuries to officers or third parties? Administrators must be able to weigh these training questions against the overall goal of reducing their liability profile.

According to most insurance companies, the biggest areas of police duty that produce liability claims are emergency vehicle operations and use of force. Why is it then that these areas fail to garner appropriate support and training? Inadequate training will likely be the predominate factor for imposing liability for excessive force actions of officers. Furthermore, it can serve as the basis for a Section 1983 liability only if the failure amounts to deliberate indifference to the right of the person whom officials encounter (City of Canton v. Harris, 1988).

Two types of situations give credence to claims of failure to train. First, the scope of duties assigned to a law enforcement officer or group may be so apparent that a failure to train would amount to deliberate indifference. Consider for example, those duties assigned to tactical teams in the jail or on the streets. The significance of force that is available and either used or not used requires a higher skill level and knowledge than duties encompassing a D.A.R.E. officer assigned to a school. Second, and relative to *Grayson v. Peed* (1999), a pattern of unconstitutional conduct may be so pervasive as to imply actual or constructive knowledge on the part of policy makers whose deliberate indifference indemnifies the individual officer, as evidenced by uncorrectable problems. The following illustrates a list of cases specific to requirements and liabilities regarding the failure to train. They may be used for reference and study where appropriate:

Turpin v. Mallet, 619 F.2d 1961 (1980)
Sager v. City of Woodland Park, 543 F.Supp. 282 (1982)

Roman v. City of Richmond, 570 F.Supp 1554 (1983)
Oklahoma City v. Tuttle, 105 S.Ct. 2427 (1985)
Voutour v. Vitale, 761 F.2nd 812 (1985)
Kibbe v. City of Springfield, 777 F.2d 801 (1985)
City of Canton v. Harris, 489 U.S. 378 (1989)

Summarily, is there a connection between training and management? Yes! Three options are clear for competence in this facet: Hire and promote officers and "hope" they work out, hire and promote those who are already proficient from the beginning, or hire and promote those with the potential to work efficiently and effectively through appropriate, congruent standards reinforced through legal and positive feedback and training. So why not train? Make it a fun, creative and constructive experience out of something that is necessary and required in the scope of criminal justice duty!

In contemporary society, professionalism has become a necessitated police response relative to the demands of both the public and police. The scope of policing is defined by broad parameters that oftentimes open law enforcement agencies to claims of criminal and civil liability. Because this scope is ambiguous and open to interpretation, identifying and implementing operational standards is of integral importance in the successful management and application of police force. Despite effective policy and procedure, training is the fulcrum of police operations. Regardless of department type, size or structure, congruencies are determined regarding the needs acquisition of police personnel. Consequently, defining and implementing organizational training standards becomes a central duty of local, state and federal training commissions.

Since the 1930s, a conscience effort has been made to promote policing as a true profession. The nature of police duty requires a substantial amount of verbal and physical communication between officers and the community they serve. Considering this, there is little doubt as to the premise of complaints, confusion, and inconsistencies regarding professional police practices. Police training is one particular action that promotes effective use of force through standards that seek to establish the best professional practices. Although a contemporary function, police training has its roots in historical contexts. From August Vollmer in Berkeley, California, to President Johnson's Commission on Law Enforcement, developing the most competent officers for public service has been a substantive task for administrators and the cornerstone of effective police duty. Since then, police officers and their agencies have succeeded in professional uses of force through educational training and vocational skills. Additionally, and within these parameters of professionalism, legal implications are central in directing police behavior. From emergency vehicle operations to use of force, contemporary standards of training are met to satisfy local, state and federal laws. Furthermore, these standards are congruent among states and regions in order to provide consistent methodologies for training.

Federal, state and local training commissions have been able to effectively define and draft training criteria that promote efficiency, effectiveness and reductions in liability lawsuits. In seeking to establish the best professional practices, standards of training regarding use of force prescribe *what* agencies should be doing, but not necessarily *how* they should be doing it. That decision is left to each police agency and their department heads through policy and procedure. Consequently, standards of use of force training are developed through a collaboration of goals relative to the needs of both the police and the community.

STANDARDS

Although achieving professional status is a priority for police agencies, it is also a problematic one as mentioned previously. In an effort to establish best police practices, officers and agencies are evaluated and scrutinized regarding the implementation of standards and their ability to adhere to them. "Acceptance by peers and the public is not given freely nor can it be purchased" (Lumb, 1994, p. 17). After all, standards are potentially embarrassing concepts, especially when this lack of adherence is publicly noticed. Consequently, a prescription of training, education and experience define the police professional and is substantiated through methods of standardization.

Definitions. Standards are statements regarding how a police organization views itself in terms of ethics, ideals, morals and principles of doing business (Lumb, 1994). Likewise, Palmiotto (1997) defined standards as a comparison of police practices against acceptable criteria through regular reviews and evaluations by a base of authority such as advisory boards. These boards often consist of individuals who are trainers or employees who have actually utilized the standards in field operations. Simply stated, standards reflect the best professional practices by providing descriptions of *what* should be accomplished in the police organization and not necessarily *how* they should be doing it. This latter task is left to the individual agency, allowing for independence and flexibility regarding methods to achieve the end result.

Scope. What exactly do police organizations seek to accomplish by the existence of standards? Gilbert (1990) explained, "The goal of standards is to ensure that all employees are prepared to function safely, securely, and effectively on the job" (p. 47). In 1979, the Commission for Accreditation of Law Enforcement Agencies (CALEA) established a body of standards to increase law enforcement capabilities relative to the prevention and control of crime (CALEA, 1998). Comprised of the IACP, the Police Executive Research Forum (PERF), the National Organization of Black Law Enforcement Executives (NOBLE) and the National Sheriff's Association (NSA), CALEA sought to improve agency effectiveness and efficiency in the delivery of law enforcement services. Furthermore, it attempted to increase cooperation with other police agencies as well as bolster community confidence in respect to agency goals, objectives and practices.

As the first organizational entity to have developed and implemented a congruent body of standards, CALEA introduced a standards manual to the law enforcement community in 1982. It wasn't until the next year that the manual was approved. Since then, the manual has been under constant review, revision and adjustment with editions being published in 1987, 1994 and 1998. As of the last publishing, the manual consisted of 439 standards covering 38 topic areas in law enforcement (CALEA,

1998). As a collection of rules and regulations, the manual provides the *minimum* requirements necessary for standard law enforcement practices. It is also utilized as a tool for agencies to govern their own operational objectives. Accreditation procedures were developed parallel to these standards as a vehicle to administer and comply with the standards. Caution should be considered, however, regarding compliance with police standards. Much like compliance of an arrested suspect, officers and agencies should never have to be limited to a single method of achievement.

Considering these implications, the manual is divided into three succinct categories: the standard statement, a commentary, and levels of compliance (CALEA, 1998). The standard statement is a declarative sentence consisting of written directories, standard operating procedures or policy statements that exist as binding contracts. Consider, for example, a written directive for the deadly use of force. Identifying conditions of the policy including "reasonable belief", "defense" or "injury", are critical terms that must be declared in writing. The commentary supports the standard but is not binding. "The commentary can serve as a prompt, as guidance to clarify the intent of the standard, or as an example of one possible way to comply with the standard" (CALEA, 1998, p. 15). Using the example of deadly force, it would be the intent of the standard to establish agency directives regarding this use as well as guidance in preventing the unnecessary loss of life. The agency is then encouraged to review the directive or make a cross-reference concerning other applicable police operations. Levels of compliance comprise the last objective in developing standard police practices. Depending upon agency size, i.e., the number of sworn personnel, administrators must determine the importance of the standard. At this point, the standard is considered mandatory, other-than-mandatory or not applicable (CALEA, 1998). Needless to say, those practices that are deemed essential for the safety of the officer must be considered mandatory. Other-than-mandatory standards are those practices that are merely "desirable". For example, conducting shift meetings may or may not be feasible each day before a tour of duty. Non-applicable standards are those that are not regulated. Consider the duty of court security or jail operations. Traditionally, the county sheriff has been responsible for this task. Therefore, a municipality would be exempt from the appropriate standards imposed upon the county agency.

Measurements. Having considered the definition and scope of standards, what is understood as sub-standard? In other words, what measurements exist that can determine whether or not an officer or criminal justice agency has met the minimum requirements necessary for safe and effective use of force in their respective duties? What do we mean by "quality" or "effective training"? How do we distinguish between a well and poorly designed training program? This process of determination can be both be objective and ambiguous. Inarguably, there exist inconsistencies regarding police selection and recruitment procedures, training programs or mere organizational commitment. In respect to training initiatives, governing bodies such as the Peace Officers Standards and Training (P.O.S.T.) have traditionally established standards without taking control over police training programs (Palmiotto, 1997). Is it likely then that this autonomy can contribute to sub-standard operations within training programs at the academy or departmental level? Consider, for example, the flexibility of use of force programs, vehicle pursuit operations, and crime scene investigations as they are trained for at the academy. Not every institution prioritizes these particular training tasks in the same context. Additionally, testing procedures to become a law enforcement officer have similar inconsistencies. Some agencies administer written, oral, psychological, physical, and polygraph examinations while other agencies administer some or none of them. Can this be considered a sub-standard practice? It is not the goal here to discuss the implications regarding the adherence to standard programming; rather, it poses a question of accountability that is so often neglected with autonomous police duty and administration.

In looking at the competence and integrity of a criminal justice agency or its officers, specific questions should be asked regarding operations and practices. Wills (1998) provided quantitative and qualitative measures as an evaluation method for determining the level of standards that are appropriate for a respective agency. There are three different perspectives that must be considered when evaluating use of force standards and operations. They are from the individual officer, the specific department and from the organization as a whole (Wills, 1998). Quantitatively, does the officer still possess the knowledge? Furthermore, are they still able to perform the skill or task? For example, one must determine if an officer is still held to the same standard of skill and performance regarding use of force as they were twenty years ago having just completed the police academy. From the departmental level, have the desired changes occurred? Has the department instituted mandatory retraining of use of force policy? Has the department increased the level of skill through appropriate continuing education measures as to allow for professional and safe use of force application? From an organizational perspective, has the goal been achieved? Does the department feel more equipped with use of force resources to fight crime? Are they safer in doing so?

From a qualitative perspective, do officers believe the training was worthwhile? Did they actually learn from the experience and believe in its premise? Departmentally, what was the reputation for the training? It is of integral importance to have quality instructors and skillful organization of the event. Furthermore, the training should meet the needs of the department. Were these particular objectives achieved? From the organizational perspective, what was the attitude towards training? Oftentimes, administrators are the purveyors of training based upon their reception of the training event. If it is not received well by them, their officers will not feel as though it was important or of sound quality. As a hierarchical, organizational event, the implications of use of force training should be understood by police administrators and distributed to their officers accordingly, based upon equitable judgment of its premise. CALEA (1998) further explained that standards relating to training should consider the organizational and administrative aspects of the training.

TRAINING

Formalized training institutions date back to the mid-nineteenth century with the New York Police Department. Known then as the "School of Instruction," police training demonstrated the most important feature of the modern-day police force (Palmiotto, 1997). With the advent of the Reform Era in the 1920s and 1930s, police training programs were concrete foundations in the larger cities of the United States. Despite these efforts, the training programs were not without criticism regarding ethical instruction, standardized operations or methods of continuous quality improvement. Since that time, training has come to embody a process of organizational effectiveness that is critical in contemporary police society.

Sullivan (1971) explained that today's police training has progressed from the time where a new recruit may have been told, "When you hit a suspect, hit him hard!" Despite the promulgation of organizational effectiveness, Holden (1994) reported that law enforcement agencies allocate less than one percent of their annual budgets to the training function. Unfortunately, this practice often leads to profiles of civil liability. In addition to Holden's findings, Stone (1994) purported that the lack of training is easily explained as a matter of economics. While training is expensive and produces time constraints, the value of training is not held in high regard, as policing is often viewed as a menial task. Is policing truly learned through normal intelligence and minimal practical application? Should it be astonishing then, that some states require more training and education of their *barbers* than of their police officers (Stone, 1994)?

Definitions. Goldstein (1974) defined training as the "systematic acquisition of skills, rules, concepts, or attitudes that results in improved performance in another environment" (p. 3). Likewise, Wills (1998) defined training as the transfer of defined and measurable knowledge or skills. In essence, they are instructional processes designed to modify human behavior. Consequently, the needs of the agency are addressed along with accountability factors, as agencies are becoming increasingly accountable for actions resulting in liability claims due to the lack of recruit or in-service training. In passing knowledge and skills to those who need them, Quinones (1997) examined the implications of Goldstein's definition and added, "training is different from learning in the sense that it is a planned set of activities that have cognitive, behavioral, or affective change as one of its goals" (p. 3). These activities are mandated by federal and state law in addition to departmental policy. Such training stipulations for police academies and in-service training programs include hours, trainer-student ratio, trainer training, trainer accreditation, delivery systems and cost (Wills, 1998).

Purposes. Wilson (1963) defined the purpose of training as a way to "make sure the officer performs all tasks with ease and in such a way as to ensure his safety and the safety and satisfaction of the public" (p. 161). Because the use of force is preceded by decisions, training must provide a background of knowledge attributable to each action. This judgment can be acquired through actual or simulated experiences or through more cognitive applications such as testing procedures (Wilson, 1963). Because no one officer is *born* with the knowledge, skills, and attitudes necessary for using force (or other practices for that matter), training is needed to improve the consistency of operations and to increase the probability that police programs will be carried out through competency, respect, legitimacy, improvement and knowledge.

Use of force is criticized on a daily basis by citizens and by police administrators. While perhaps constructive, this criticism can become negative as a result of officers not knowing *how* to use force during the course of duty. An officer's lack of preparedness to handle situations is not always indicative of their individual transgressions. Although some laws are changing, many states require that an officer attend a basic training academy within one year of their employment as a police officer (Stone, 1994). During this time, however, officers are working the street untrained, unaware of liability and posing a significant, potential danger to the community. In defense of this statement, however, many departments are at the mercy of the training academy regarding "slots" available upon the appointment of their officers. Consequently, administrators tend to alleviate this pressure by assigning new recruits to a field-training officer until a slot becomes available.

The use of field training officers, while beneficial and prudent, does not eliminate the need of administrators to account for liability regarding the lack of officer certification during this waiting period. Another cause related to the need of training is based upon the decision of administrators to rely only on their state's minimum training requirements (Stone, 1994). Unfortunately, these minimum standards only afford the officer the "nuts and bolts" of police operations. As a result, departments fail to implement training programs that meet modern curricula or establish trained trainers. Too often, considerations for training are based upon immediate public needs, demographic conditions or the "hot topic" in crime. Therefore, while a five-officer, rural agency is training for gang violence, such procedures as use of force and emergency vehicle operations are being neglected. Despite research that indicates a congruent set of police operations and crime problems, why is training not met to satisfy these needs?

Holden (1994) identified four particular factors that assist in answering this question and further substantiates the purpose for training. They are social evolution, legal mandates, maximizing performance and prolonging employee service. Without training, the best an officer can be is inadequate and at the worst, incompetent.

Social evolution. Social evolution is the first element that necessitates the need for use of force training. Obviously, policing is different today than it was twenty years ago. As a result, agencies must change with the changing times. Social trends dictate the need for adequate training (Holden, 1994). While the 1960s and 1970s focused on firearms and the physical manageability for offender compliance, contemporary police duty requires more social skills. Understanding human behavior including emotions, reactions and attitudes, helps the law enforcement officer discern which response is appropriate in effecting a specific force option. Wilson (1963) further explained this premise by stating, "...the accomplishment of the police purpose necessitates a control of people that is best effected by winning their compliance with laws and ordinances" (p. 161). This task, however, is easier said than done. Conflicts arise within the police agency because of age and experience discrepancies. Although it is not the goal to denigrate senior officers in this context, it must be reasonably understood that the adage of teaching an "old dog new tricks" is somewhat legitimate. "While nothing can substitute for experience, not all officers learn from their mistakes and many are unwilling to admit old practices are failures" (Holden, 1994, p. 282). In all fairness, however, new recruits expel similar stubbornness regarding the acquisition of new techniques, tactics or philosophies.

Legal mandates. The second factor posed by Holden (1994) is legal mandates. Becoming a "mini-lawyer" is an appropriate response to the mere definition of law enforcement. Being constantly aware of new laws and legal procedures in the use of force is of integral importance in the training process. More importantly perhaps, is the acquisition of knowledge regarding civil liability (Holden, 1994). Although police officers enforce criminal laws, they are often subject to civil litigation in respect to inappropriate uses of force. Liability has always existed as somewhat of a checks and balance system. Civil litigation has increased in frequency, however, to the point where officers and agencies spend more time and money defending themselves instead of their community. As a remedy in reducing a department's profile in spite of litigious activity, administrators must be aware of this propensity and implement satisfactory training measures to ensure appropriate use of force practices are met.

Maximizing performance. Maximizing performance is the third factor examined by Holden (1994). Without training, officers are completely independent. With training, they are armed with better judgment and discretionary capabilities. While policies and procedures provide equitable guidance, they are also impersonal and oftentimes vague. "Training is the most certain method of instilling organizational values and pride in the individual officer" (Holden, 1994, p. 284).

Prolonging service. The last factor, prolonging employee service, comprises the most problematic effort for use of force training. Several aspects of policing create frustrations that training may or may not be able to alleviate. Holden (1994) explained that one particular reason for officer turnover is due to the bureaucratic structure of the organization. "Too many chiefs and not enough Indians," is a common phrase throughout corporate America. In addition to the myriad of policies and procedures that inundate this environment, officers must deal with middle management stifling their suggestions and creative thoughts regarding best police practices.

Another frustration comes from the inability of the court system and law enforcement to work together. The role of the police and the courts is ambiguous and cause tension because of the substantive principles of law, i.e., making future decisions based upon past decisions of a similar nature. In addition to the court system, the mere nature of policing causes frustrations and officer turnover. This aspect is more open to interpretation, as it includes not only the officer but the officer's family as well. Furthermore, solvability factors of crime, poor pay, shift work and potential violence are all factors of policing that compound frustrations.

What is it that training can provide to cure these repressive ills? Regarding management, Holden (1994) explained that training could alleviate the need for restrictive supervision. Although the chief administrator has allocated responsibility elsewhere, a properly trained middle manager can more effectively do his job, which, in turn, creates a more favorable environment for those in the lower ranks. In respect to the court system, training provides a less-insular outlook regarding the duties of the court system, as known qualities are less frustrating than unknown ones. Last, alleviating the nature of policing elicits problematic training efforts. To change this nature means changing the entire scope of policing and this task is virtually impossible. Training can provide an understanding of job limitations before they become frustrations (Holden, 1994).

Training Programs

Understanding how training programs work (or don't work) and whether or not they meet the minimum standard training requirements, may better serve the police administrator in developing use of force training programs that satisfy the needs of their officers. This is achieved not only through the scope of legal parameters but also through a critical examination of curricula that is applicable to every law enforcement officer.

Police academy

Police academies, as the foundation of police training, have traditionally encompassed the military style of organization and instruction. As a paramilitary structure, police academies seek to integrate knowledge through discipline and acquiescence. Law and procedure, firearms and self-defense, often illustrate criteria within this method of organization. Most administrators and academy directors have expressed that the military model works because of its historical successes and the contemporary implications of policing that require quick decision-making and judgments in the field. Holden (1994) disagreed with this model by explaining that military-oriented police academies are archaic and dysfunctional. He expressed that creativity and imagination are repressed due to this organization and ultimately inhibits the officer's growth towards professionalism. He further explained, "The better approach to police training is designed along lines similar to the college experience. Training is provided through a variety of techniques, but the salient feature is the positive environment provided for learning" (Holden, 1994, p. 286). Having provided these modalities, a critical analysis of the police academy may be explored to identify problems and solutions in respect to use of force training curricula and its standards.

All state legislatures in the United States, as executed through a review body such as training commissions, are required to establish and certify all training academies. Furthermore, they are to establish a minimum curriculum and evaluate the training facilities on a continual basis (Palmiotto, 1997). There are three different types of police academies that exist in this country: agency, regional, and college-sponsored. Large municipal agencies often establish their own academies in an effort to "train their own" regarding socialization and department-specific skills and operations (Thibault, 1998). By contrast, regional academies exist in greater quantities for the purpose of training an entire area within a state. They, too, train larger departments; however, most states are comprised of smaller agencies within a large geographic area. College-sponsored academies are operated on the premise of post-secondary institutions such as community colleges and four-year universities. These institutes allow police officers to obtain college credit while pursuing law enforcement certification. Regardless of the method of training, each state mandates curricula that are congruent among all academies in the country. Selecting use of force curricula for a police academy is a difficult task. It requires yearly review and evaluation in order to change with the changing times, therefore meeting the needs of officers and the public.

Physical harm. Since almost all criminal justice work is predicated on decision-making, it is only reasonable to expect that use of force curricula be established that minimizes harm to officers and the public by maximizing decision-making efforts. Life and death decisions must be a training priority in academy curriculum development due to the legal power of deadly force held by law enforcement officers. Holden (1994) explained that academy and departmental curricula should consider laws, agency policies, and proper decision-making regarding the use of deadly force. For example, the Kansas Law Enforcement Training Center in Hutchinson, KS currently allocates 74 hours of the 400 hours required to become state-certified as a full-time law enforcement officer for use of force training (KLETC, 2001). This training includes legal parameters of force usage and proficiency methods of firearms, defensive tactics and handcuffing. Although firearms proficiency comprises the majority of the academy use of force training experience in America, it also serves as an appropriate illustration regarding the inherent problems many police academies and departments encounter with training in other aspects of force.

Shenkman (1984) conducted a study that explained a lack of strategies by United States police agencies and academies regarding the training measures to promote deadly force decision-making and firearms proficiency. Although dated by almost twenty years, this study constitutes training factors that are still disregarded in contemporary training programs. For example, many police academies and agencies do not require low-light shooting; despite evidence that most armed confrontations occur during nighttime hours. Secondly, few academies use multiple selection and moving targets to promote proper targeting and quick decision-making (Shenkman, 1984). Third, only 20 percent of police agencies use service ammunition for firearms training. Although that percentage has certainly increased, a number of departments currently utilize practice ammunition of a lower caliber to alleviate expense and increase target proficiency. This practice, however, contributes to ill-preparedness regarding the noise, kick, and trajectory of service ammunition in a combat situation (Shenkman, 1984). From these results, one can observe the need for prioritizing an appropriate firearms curriculum. With it, a police officer's mental and physical capacity may be tested, as it is brought together with the utilization of weapons and deadly force decision-making. "The situation, the law, department policy, the officer's values, and firearms training, must all come together at the same time" (Holden, 1994, p. 289).

Legal actions. Legal actions comprise another priority topic of academy curriculum development. Police authority and power constitute a profound impact on citizens who are affected by it (Holden, 1994). For example: handcuffing; while a menial task to the law enforcement officer, can yield disastrous results if the implications are not understood by all of the parties involved. Financial burdens, public humiliation and embarrassment are all results of inappropriate police actions, which subsequently necessitate the need for appropriate training measures to instill the best professional police practices.

Routine decisions. Because law enforcement operates under the large umbrella of order maintenance, many tasks of the police are considered "routine". Holden (1994) explained, "The training program should strive to identify those functions within the agency that are common occurrences and teach the officer the most appropriate method of response" (p. 291). Use of force training allows for discussions and feedback relative to certain common situations and circumstances. Furthermore, new techniques can be adapted rapidly to changes in environments. Whether handcuffing a wanted suspect or quelling a verbal dispute, officers are better equipped to handle these situations with use of force training that addresses specific needs.

Skill enhancement. As a professional objective, police officers should be able to think critically and be articulate in verbal and written communications. Although this skill is performed enough in day-to-day operations to constitute practice or routine, teaching the basics allows for necessary skills to foster increasing capabilities (Holden, 1994). Many prosecutors fail to proceed with charges in criminal cases because of poorly written police reports. Despite a plethora of evidence mounted against a suspect, incompetent communication reflects poor police practices and a lack of professionalism that is ultimately exhibited through officer testimony.

In-service

In-service training is another program in addition to the police academy. More controversy exists with in-service training, however, due to the latitude regarding training curriculum. Also called mandatory retraining, annual training, or continuing education, in-service was adopted in 1914 by the New York City Police Department. At that time, it was recognized that senior law enforcement personnel needed to be retrained on laws, procedures, and regulations in an effort to keep apprised of new changes in policing (Palmiotto, 1997). Since the end of World War II, mandatory retraining has been a requirement of every law enforcement agency as a means of increasing officer proficiency. It is currently required by state law in order to maintain police certification. For example, the Kansas Law Enforcement Training Center (2001) stipulated that any officer who fails to complete forty hours of in-service training will be suspended without pay until those hours are completed. After a certain period of time without compliance, an officer could lose his police certification.

As a continuous quality improvement method, Wilson (1963) provided that in-service training should cater to changes in departmental policies, adaptation to new techniques and ultimately to "fill the gap" in respect to weaknesses in the basic training curriculum. As a means of increasing officer efficiency, in-service training seeks to establish best practices through training programs evaluated by an agency's existing operations (Stone, 1994). Consequently, the needs of police officers may be determined. For example, if a large quantity of traffic citations is being dismissed in court, it might be the result of technical errors in police procedure. Addressing this problem with appropriate training not only satisfies hourly requirements for in-service, but promotes efficiency and effectiveness in the police operation. The controversy regarding curriculum, however, is apparent when analyzing the agency's demographics and roles. "An officer can be in the field for several years in a small agency and never encounter a situation calling for competent training" (Holden, 1994, p. 293). As a result, the quality of training is sporadic, as agencies are unable to discern definitive needs. Depending on specific regions of a state, some officers may receive exceptional training while others will not.

Education
Since the inception of college-educated officers in 1920, the controversy regarding its value as the pinnacle of proficiency and professionalism continues into the contemporary police society. As a broad, theoretical focus, criminal justice education seeks to involve the student-officer in creative, critical thinking applications of the larger social system. It also includes understanding the historical contexts of the discipline. To differentiate the premise of education and training, consider, for example, the operation of a breath alcohol instrument. An officer could be trained to operate the instrument without understanding the basic foundation of the machine. Likewise, the officer could learn the history and theory of the instrument without being shown specifically how it works. Both methods, however, are important and end up being synthesized into training modules that police

officers learn at the academy or in-service training functions. In this context, the officer is both educated and trained.

A background in such occupational concepts is not necessarily the argument regarding education as a training component; rather, education is most often discussed as a college degree initiative. According to Palmiotto (1997), the LEAA's consensus in 1967 was that, "...in order to improve law enforcement, the quality of police personnel had to be upgraded through education" (p. 258). Sapp and Carter (1992) conducted research to justify the attributes of a college education as an indication of professional police practice as well as an equitable training mechanism for police personnel. They found that officers with college degrees had a greater appreciation of their professional role, exhibited interpersonal skills, and possessed behavioral attributes including empathy and initiative. Palmiotto (1997) concurred by stating, "Higher education exposes students to ideas, concepts, and problem-solving techniques" (p. 258). Conversely, O'Rourke (1971) determined that many good officers did not necessarily possess college degrees. In his research, a degree often contributed to boredom for a police officer, ultimately leading to turnover for the department. Consequently, smaller police agencies had difficulty in competitively recruiting college graduates. Requiring a college education for police officers in accordance with training standards posed a particular problem for departments in respect to minorities. Because recruitment of minorities was difficult based upon a lack of education, this violated the Civil Rights Act of 1964 (O'Rourke, 1971).

Delivery. With the dawn of the Information Age, society faces new challenges in regard to learning. Whether it is corporate training or a college education, the increasing demands of the global work force require an appropriate adaptation by human service professionals. Police agencies are at the heart of this transition, as technological advances have required a reorganization of training methods. Why is the delivery of police training important? In an effort to establish standardization through best professional practices, methods of delivery must be examined to evaluate the scope of learning in accordance with state law. A plethora of topics and police officers makes this scope problematic, as certain curricula is based upon skill and technique while others are based upon only cognitive applications.

Lecture. Lecture styles of police training are the most popular and have traditionally afforded the greatest opportunity for skill acquisition. "Lecture is a very cost-effective method for conveying information to a large group of people" (Holden, 1994, p. 294). Firearms training, defensive tactics and other use of force programs are at the foreground of lecture-oriented, face-to-face training environments. Hands-on applications may be appropriately instructed and supervised, allowing for an equitable amount of feedback from the trainee. A particular downfall with this training environment is getting a large number of participants together at the same time. Furthermore, a difficult task is sustaining their attention over the course of training. Few questions are raised, however, regarding the standards applied to this delivery method. Proper skills can be acquired through written and proficiency examinations by the trainer. Not only does this indicate satisfactory or unsatisfactory accomplishment, it allows for a longer retention of the knowledge obtained.

Television. "Distance education can be a useful tool in meeting the demands inherent to law enforcement in-service training programs" (Austen-Kern, 2001). Consider, for example, rotating shifts, weekends, and days off. Distance education programs meet the needs of officers by making instructional times convenient. Interactive television is a contemporary tool that is used to reach beyond the traditional classroom setting. Utilized by both academies and colleges, this method of delivery introduces "question and answer" sessions that promote creative thinking and insightful commentary among students and student-officers. Thibault (1997) explained that the Law Enforcement Training Network (LETN) affords interactive police training through an actual schedule of training events. A police agency may choose the topics they desire and pay for the service accordingly. Other audiovisual methods in addition to interactive television include the use of videotapes. In an effort to alleviate time and location constraints with lectures or interactive television, videos are an inexpensive and individualized form of instruction. This is a valuable asset for officers who miss training dates due to illness, family responsibilities or time off. It also offers easy access to training topics for simple review purposes.

The premise of interactive television or videos as training methods is problematic regarding the quality of certain skills or techniques. This is of integral importance to the police administrator regarding liability issues in training. Some departments are satisfied with a four-hour instructional video on such defensive tactics techniques as ground fighting. Although the video may exhibit proper techniques and practices while counting for in-service training hours, it does *not* constitute skill proficiency by any means. As a result, many trainers today are utilizing videos and television in *conjunction* with face-to-face training environments to promote a synthesis of learning. To learn the philosophical and theoretical foundations of a skill are appropriate when followed by demonstrations and testing that contribute to the officer's level of skill.

Web-based. While it is not the solution for every problem, web-based training is the fastest growing method in police education and training programs today. It is a prolific and valuable method for teaching particular police skills. The computer provides a supplement to the college education, academy experience, or in-service training curriculum where cognitive skills are specifically needed. Applications of use of force procedures and problem-solving techniques comprise some of the cognitive skills necessary for police personnel that are offered on the web. In determining the scope of web-based training however, Driscoll (1998) explained that, "It will not work if the performance problem is the result of factors other than lack of skill or knowledge" (p. 2). For example, psychomotor skills instructed in firearms and defensive tactics training require a combination of gross and fine motor skills that obviously cannot be taught over the computer. Additionally, reinforcement strategies and behavioral skills cannot be applied over the Internet without having reduced some degree of quality. While this delivery method reduces travel time, costs and the problems associated with packaging and mailing videotapes, web-based curricula lack a range of attributable skills and variety in police topics. Furthermore, not every police agency in the United States meets full compliance regarding the resources to utilize these methods of delivery.

Professionalism and best practices have been reiterated on numerous occasions throughout this text. Based upon the successes and failures of police history and considering the inevitable changes that occur in contemporary society, today's law enforcement officer must be prepared to meet societal threats with the proper response. Furthermore, the police are to effectively work with the community they serve under undesirable conditions. Training and training standards promote these professional police practices through a congruent set of goals, values, and principles that should be recognized in every police agency and academy. While many officers and administrators are intimidated by new standards, they surround every aspect of daily life. Before deciding whether or not a police officer and agency deserve the most prolific and efficient means of training, consider whether or not one would knowingly purchase a home with electrical systems that failed to meet the required construction codes. Or how much one would enjoy dining at a restaurant that failed a recent health inspection. Regardless of the scenario, training and standards provide a reasonable level of reliability: *quality*, *certainty* and *security* that are critical to effectively work as a law enforcement officer.

SCOPE OF USE OF FORCE TECHNIQUES

In the business of use of force, only one principle is static for trainers, administrators, and criminal justice practitioners: the law. This "law" encompasses everything from federal use of force to administrative guidelines and use of force continuums. What is most often open to interpretation, however, is the use of force techniques that professionals should use in performing their duties under the color of law.

For many years, much "squabbling" has occurred in procuring the best model of success for achieving proficiency in armed and unarmed conflicts. With a lack of congruent defensive tactics and firearm programs at the academy level, and an ever-increasing field of commercial use of force systems, discerning a certain and appropriate use of force program for a department has become difficult. More importantly, many programs have failed to recognize the basic principles that define and substantiate the use of force: control and self-defense. In the quest for marketability, these principles have become clouded through techniques not applicable to the officer's environment, a lack of situational training, and through unqualified use of force instructors. As a result, not only is the safety and security of officers and the public in jeopardy, but administrators have a difficult time getting their prosecutors "on board" when it's time to review use of force incidences that result in injuries and litigation.

Because most unarmed defensive tactics techniques, specifically, are based upon the martial arts, they were not originally designed for arresting suspects. Therefore, techniques must be field tested and modified for street and jail applications. Summarily, whether using the weaver or isosceles stance when firing a weapon or using a jiujitsu move in subduing a suspect, two variables must be understood and trained for: control and self-defense. If trainers and administrators can clarify training objectives through this scope, then climbing the ladder of success becomes easier in using justifiable force.

As mentioned previously, use of force is a dynamic situation. Officers are constantly moving back and forth between control and self-defense. There is a very fine line when circumstances warrant both aspects within seconds of each other. Control can be defined as a degree of influence that an officer exerts over another in responding to a problem. Interestingly enough, officers must not only control the subject but themselves as well. Both self control and control of violators, as purveyors of successful outcomes, is developed by skills received through training and practice. The goal of subject control is to gain compliance or cooperation in effecting an arrest or other circumstances leading to a lawful detention.

Techniques and technologies in subject control baffle the everyday officer when definitive guidelines and application principles are not understood. For example, many control techniques lead to pain responses if executed with subject resistance. Continuing or exceeding these responses are often problem areas for many officers in executing control techniques. Pepper sprays and less-lethal devices, which are functional and necessary, do not control individuals but subdue them and incapacitate them to the point that physical control can be established. When considering control, one must consider physical control. While officers are never "out of the woods" in respect to potential attacks, a controlled violator is a safely and legally restrained one. Thus, restrained individuals are *physically* placed into restraint devices, *physically* removed from a premise and so forth. Control should also be utilized with the element of surprise. Combining this element with affirmative and decisive application of the proper control technique will allow officers to control effectively and efficiently. Physical confrontations with subjects that rely on strength and stamina can be averted, reducing the chance of physical injury to the officer or subject.

Law enforcement officers are taught early in their careers that they must gain control over any situation they are called to. Unfortunately, they are not provided with the tools to accomplish this task. Actions are based upon equipment and training. Eliminating or not providing either not only increases the chances of injury or death but also increases the chances for negligent actions on the part of the law enforcement officer. While pain compliance tools, for example, are effective, they are so in certain situations. They most often fail to work on intoxicated and inebriated individuals. Furthermore, they are not designed to control but to serve as a distraction technique or as an application to be used in conjunction with a control measure.

Several challenges currently face use of force trainers in respect to selling, establishing, and implementing control techniques and programs in their departments. First, good control techniques should be designed so that a single officer working alone can subdue and handcuff a violator. Secondly, techniques should be a gross motor skill that is easy to learn, easy to use, and easy to remember. Third, officers must feel confident in the technique and their ability to perform with it. Last, control techniques should complement other training they have previously received. If the departmental training staff and administrators can accomplish all of these variables, officers will receive quality use of force training and techniques and be able to reduce vicarious liability.

As the second principle of use of force, self-defense or "self-protection" carries significant implications in the dynamics of using force. An officer must be able to recognize and interpret a tense and evolving situation and make quick decisions regarding the magnitude of such event. In other words, if an officer is not controlling or attempting to control a violator and is instead preparing to defend himself or others, they must decide the level of self-protection to employ. Is this merely a case of a simple deflection technique or must the officer draw his firearm and shoot? The more skills that an officer can learn and retain will provide numerous options that can protect the officer or others. Why limit them? Additionally, it is of integral importance for trainers and administrators to review their use of force incidences and research those areas of incident that require certain measures in protection. While a plethora of techniques in self-defense exist, it is the ultimate responsibility of the trainer and administrator to seek out and promote the best option for their agency and furthermore, not limit their department to necessarily one commercially available system.

CLAMP™ and GRASP™

Numerous control and self-defense systems exist in contemporary police use of force training programs. As mentioned previously, it is important for the trainer and administrator to choose those programs which have high retention rates and are applicable to all police encounters with combative subjects. Any use of force training program should have the following elements:

Work in the real world
Reasonable amount of time to learn

Agency, courts, and local community must accept it
Must have acceptable costs
Training techniques must be integrated into patrol tactics
Legal parameters must be identified and understood
Basis of testing (documentation)

The CLAMP™ and GRASP™ programs created by L.E.S.T., Inc. comprise such variables offered in a control and self-defense program. Of critical importance within these programs are defining the premise for which the techniques are to be utilized. Outside of the general, large law enforcement and correctional settings, most departments are comprised of smaller city and sheriff's offices throughout the country. These officers are often the only ones on duty and may not have the option of calling a backup officer. These lone officers are faced with the possibility of having to subdue, control, and handcuff a subject by themselves. Considering this, it is imperative that these officers have training in a control technique which is easy to learn, easy to employ and can be retained with minimum practice, and when utilized, will allow them to arrest, control and handcuff a subject by themselves. Most officers, however, have difficulty in utilizing empty-hand techniques because of the skills required for application or the lack of practice of the technique(s).

CLAMP™ is an acronym for the Chris Lein Arm Management Program. It was created in 1989 to rectify a weakness in the area of subject control, specifically for use with a belligerent or resistive subject being arrested by one officer. The technical basis of the CLAMP™ is taken from the Ude Garami (bent armlock) which is commonly used in the martial arts discipline of Judo as a submission hold in mat or groundwork. The technique is executed to both destabilize the attacker and cause the shoulder to rotate until compliance is gained by submission. Furthermore, it emphasizes control with the application of body mechanics and does not rely on pain compliance to be effective. The CLAMP™ serves as an additional tool which law enforcement and correctional officers may use to control and handcuff an arrested or resistive subject. The technique fits into the force continuum starting at soft-empty hand techniques or with passive resistance (depending on policy).

GRASP™, or Ground Reaction and Self-Protection, encompasses those principles as stated previously under self-defense. These two systems work excellently together, as they provide mechanisms under the auspice of force dynamics. Most research in the field suggests that over 60 percent of officer assaults end up on the ground. Although fighting on the ground has been with mankind since its inception, only recently has it been acknowledged in police training. While on the ground, many officers are put into situations where they are at a tactical disadvantage and cannot disengage from the violator. At this point, the officer should be concerned with self-defense first and control second. Ideally, officers should avoid groundfighting situations. They should attempt to ground a subject for control, if necessary, without going to the ground to fight with them. Consider that mobility is limited, weapon protection is increasingly difficult and body weight and strength is a factor. Groundfighting is a survival issue and this is explicitly expressed in the GRASP™ program. L.E.S.T., Inc. (1996) provided seven basic principles an officer should recognize in groundfighting situations:

- Do not panic! With training, you have experience.
- Relax and breathe. If you suffer from oxygen depletion, your knowledge and skill will be of little value after 30-50 seconds.
- Be aware of the positional relationship of your weapon to the subject. Remember that getting your weapon may be their only goal.
- Stay in a face-to-face relative position with the subject. Don't turn your back to him.
- Use your feet and legs to help control the subject.
- React to opportunities given to you by the subject.
- Think "round" when you go to the ground. Tuck in your chin and roll.

Officers need to remember that the objective of groundfighting is to gain control of the subject and get back onto their feet. The GRASP™ program addresses those needs and offers alternatives to losing a groundfighting encounter.

LESS-THAN-LETHAL TECHNOLOGIES

Along with armed and unarmed use of force strategies, a concern over civil liability as an agent for change has further necessitated the need and implementation of less-than-lethal technologies. In addition to the actual numbers of civil litigation cases that have increased in recent years, the *fears* of liability as driven by such Supreme Court decisions as *Tennessee v. Garner* (1985) and *Graham v. Connor* (1989) have promoted the development of less aggressive policies with respect to apprehension and care. The recent progression has thus moved towards a battery of less-than-lethal tactics and technologies as a contemporary means of force usage by many criminal justice entities. From rubber bullets to pepper spray, numerous technologies exist, and continue to be proffered, in an effort to promote the best techniques and tactics available to safely and effectively use force.

Despite the effectiveness of such tactics, several issues and constraints have hampered the ability for less-than-lethal technologies to be embraced as a prominent force strategy in the scope of criminal justice duty. These issues were raised by a report from the United States Attorney General (1987) on less-than-lethal weapons:

Reasons to Continue Development:

1. Avoid serious injury and death of fleeing felons.
2. Decrease the number of law enforcement officers shot with their own weapons.
3. Provide adequate force options.
4. Respond more effectively to disturbed and/or violent perpetrators.
5. Lessen the number of lawsuits involving police officers.

Issues and Constraints:

1. Since any force that is used against an individual can be potentially lethal, acceptable limits of potential risk must be set.
2. The design of a new device should incorporate features to limit the potential for abuse.
3. The participation of biomedical experts is critical in order to clarify the physiological effects and consequences of new weapons.
4. Acceptance of the officers using the weapon is critical.
5. Administrative controls for actual use should be considered in development.
6. Devices must not be overly complex; they must be durable and simple for the officer to use, but potentially difficult for others to use.
7. The delivery system must be at least as accurate as a conventional handgun.

Funding problems and scope of agency size are also determinants in the acceptability of less-than-lethal force strategies. While the National Institute of Justice has provided statistics regarding the general nature of budgets with department size (Seaskate, Inc., 1998), a survey by the Police Executive Research Forum in 1996 found that procurement of less-than-lethal force options were inhibited by mere cost of the technology no matter how large or small the department (Weisheit, 1999). Furthermore, the application for state and federal grants to assist in procuring such force technology is, to say the least, unpredictable.

COMPREHENSIVE USE OF FORCE TRAINING MODEL

In 2001, I revised an original draft of what I considered to be a model of "best practices" in respect to use of force training in my home state of Kansas. It is intended to be a comprehensive and explicit display of learning objectives when engaged in in–service training. For purposes of officer competency and administrative control documentation, this model assists in developing and enforcing written policy, education, and annual training in the use of force. The learning objectives serve as a "road map" that, once determined, allows the inclusion of a lesson plan built around those goals and objectives. It can be used and modified to your own state laws and administrative policy:

Learning Objectives

Foreword
Use of Force
Readiness Aspects of Use of Force
Proficiency with Unarmed Control Measures
Proficiency with Intermediate Force Weapons
Principles of Firearms Usage
Handgun Range Exercises
Other Firearms Range Exercises
Firearm Selection
Use of Firearms in Low Light and in Adverse Weather

FOREWORD

This model has been developed to assist law enforcement and related agencies in providing use of force in-service training to agency officers. Training officers and agency administrators should be aware of the following information:

There are many forms of completing in-service training, e.g., multi-media, face-to-face, agency host, etc.

It is recognized that individual officers have different levels of ability; additionally, there are individual differences among law enforcement agencies throughout the state of Kansas. Therefore, the agency must determine the minimum competency levels appropriate for agency personnel, consistent with accepted competency levels based upon the duty and nature of operations.

Nothing in these objectives prohibits an agency from developing additional objectives, requiring higher standards or developing alternative means of testing an officer's knowledge, understanding and competency. This allows the agency to provide meaningful education that meets the needs and abilities of the officer, the agency and the community.

It is intended that officers receive instruction relative only to weapons and equipment that the officer is issued or authorized to use, i.e., handcuffs, mace, baton, firearms, empty-hand control, etc.

USE OF FORCE

General learning goal:

The officer will explain the criteria that are used to determine when force may be employed, the circumstances that justify the use of deadly force or non-deadly force, and the liabilities attached to the use of force.

Performance Objectives:

The officer will identify and explain the federal statutes that authorize and govern the use of reasonable force.

The officer will identify and explain the two instances in which Kansas Statute K.S.A. 21-3215 authorizes an officer to use reasonable force.

The officer will review and explain the agency's policy regarding the use of force.

The officer will explain why federal, state, and administrative laws regarding the use of force are important.

The officer will explain the Federal Use of Force Continuum, how it should be utilized, and why the continuum is not always linear. The following concepts should be discussed:

Officer Presence
Verbal Skills
Empty-hand control (soft & hard)
Intermediate Weapons (including non-lethal)
Deadly Force

The officer will demonstrate knowledge of the circumstances under federal and state law in which a peace officer may use deadly force.

The officer will demonstrate familiarity with the agency's policy concerning the use of deadly force.

The officer will explain the criminal, civil, and administrative consequences of unlawful or unreasonable use of force.

READINESS ASPECTS OF USE OF FORCE

General learning goal:

The officer will explain the importance of mental and physical readiness, and the necessity for post-critical incident trauma evaluation relative to the use of force.

Performance Objectives:

The officer will explain how extremely stressful situations will affect physical and mental functioning. The explanation must cover the following:

- Breathing and circulation
- Changes in sensory perception
- Changes in motor skills
- Physical trauma

The officer will identify the symptoms of "critical incident trauma" and discuss the need for evaluating and treating their effects, to include:

- Sleep disturbances
- Emotional distancing
- Hyper-alertness or exaggerated startle response
- Memory impairment or trouble concentrating
- Inability to express feelings

The officer will explain the concept of "post-shooting trauma" and discuss the agency's response to officers involved in deadly force and other critical incidents.

The officer will explain the concept that people can have varying responses when force, including deadly force, is applied.

PROFICIENCY WITH
UNARMED CONTROL MEASURES

General learning goal:

The officer will demonstrate proficiency and explain the importance of unarmed control measures which the officer is certified to use and/or authorized by the officer's agency to use.

Performance Objectives:

The officer will demonstrate proficiency in the following areas:

- Verbalization/command skills
- Handcuffing (or other restraining devices)
- Weapon retention
- Empty hand techniques (variable; for control or self-defense)

The officer will explain situations that would cause an excessive use of force in each of the above areas.

Proficiency in the above areas are examined by prior education and training, current education and training, documentation of written tests, physical tests, etc.

PROFICIENCY WITH
INTERMEDIATE FORCE WEAPONS

General learning goal:

The officer will discuss and demonstrate proficiency with the various intermediate weapons used by the agency.

Performance Objectives:

If the officer is issued or authorized to carry and use chemical aerosols, impact weapons, specialty impact munitions, electronic weapons, or other intermediate weapons, the officer will demonstrate proficiency in the use of these weapons consistent with agency policy(s).

The officer will explain situations that would cause an excessive use of force in each of the above areas.

Proficiency in the above areas are examined by prior education and training, current education and training, documentation of written tests, physical tests, etc.

PRINCIPLES OF FIREARMS USE

General learning goal:

During the course of practical firearms training, the officer will demonstrate knowledge of firearms safety, firearms maintenance, handgun shooting principles and familiarization with authorized firearms. This training will be consistent with agency policies and individual officer assignments.

Performance Objectives:

The officer will demonstrate safe handling of all firearms used during training. This will include:

- Safely and correctly loading and unloading firearms
- Safely and correctly holstering and drawing firearms
- Safely and correctly clearing malfunctions
- Safely and correctly maintaining authorized firearms

The officer will identify authorized firearms categories and corresponding ammunition utilized by the agency.

The officer will explain situations in which use of the weak hand may be required.

The officer will explain the circumstances that justify the use of deadly force by peace officers.

HANDGUN RANGE EXERCISES

General learning goal:

Any officer who is issued or is authorized to carry a handgun will effectively and safely utilize the authorized handgun(s) on a qualification course of fire.

Performance Objectives:

The officer will demonstrate effective techniques in the following areas:

-Close encounter shooting
-Shooting from cover
-Reloading techniques
-Weapon/reaction hand shooting

The following will be determined by the department rangemaster; however, a general outline will be given regarding exercises.

The officer will fire a qualification course consisting of no less than 50 rounds. During the course of fire, the officer's issued service ammunition will be fired.

During the course of fire, the officer will fire from close, medium and long range. Close range is less than 7 yards; medium range 7 to 14 yards; and long range 15 to 25 yards. (Suggested use of ammunition allotment: 50% at close range; 40% at medium range and 10% at long range.)

The agency will determine the minimum proficiency to be obtained for successful completion of the exercise.

OTHER FIREARMS RANGE EXERCISES

General learning goal:

Any officer who is authorized to use other firearms (shotgun, rifle, AR-15, etc.) will effectively and safely utilize these firearms in a qualification course of fire.

Performance Objectives:

Given a qualification course of fire, the officer will successfully complete the following:

At varying distances, the officer will demonstrate proficiency in the use of other firearms which the officer is authorized to use.

The officer will fire the weapon(s) from varying distances. The officer will also observe the shot pattern and dispersal of rounds, which result from the deviations of distance.

The officer will fire a minimum of 10 rounds during the exercise.

The agency will determine the minimum proficiency to be obtained for successful completion of the exercise.

FIREARM SELECTION

General learning goal:

The officer will identify the situations or considerations involved in determining which firearm (handgun or other firearm) is appropriate in various tactical situations.

Performance Objectives:

The officer will identify important considerations when deciding which firearm should be used in a tactical situation, to include:

the physical environment
the number of suspect(s)
the weapons available to suspect(s)
the presence of bystanders, hostages, or other innocent persons
the presence and deployment of assisting officers
the officer's level of training with authorized weapons
the firearms policy of the agency
the potential for ricochet, projectile pattern and projectile penetration

The officer will describe and compare the recognized or effective range of various firearms authorized by the agency.

USE OF FIREARMS IN LOW LIGHT AND IN ADVERSE WEATHER

General learning goal:

The officer will demonstrate the ability to deal with the special problems associated with the use of firearms in low light and in adverse weather.

Performance Objectives:

The officer will demonstrate the ability to deal with the following problems associated with use of authorized firearms in low light:

muzzle flash
target identification
target accuracy

The officer will demonstrate the ability to solve the following problems associated with adverse weather conditions:

firearm malfunction
firearm control
use of gloves
reduced mobility in drawing and firing the handgun due to heavy clothing
limitation of access to handguns due to heavy outer clothing
impact of cold weather in reducing motor function of the extremities.

REPORT WRITING

We've all heard the term, "the more you fight, the more you write." This is not at all far from the truth. Sound report writing in the use of force is analogous to comfort whereby comfort equals a continuity of police action without fear. In a litigious society, where essentially *any* action may find you sued, it is critical to have accurate and concise documentation of events as they happened as well as how the officer perceived the event. With three to five years on a statute of limitations, an officer may not remember an arrest, or the events surrounding the arrest, but the plaintiff will. Furthermore, they will have witnesses, medical reports and other documents that can stand the test of time.

There should be two types of reports following a use of force incident: a use of force report form or what should be called a "subject resistance form" (see figure 3.15), and a comprehensive narrative, much like any narrative written following an investigation of a crime. The form should be a brief checklist that denotes circumstances that can be articulated for immediate and initial review and can be used as a foundation and reference for the narrative. In reporting a use of force incident in narrative form, it is important for the officer to clearly provide details of the event from beginning to end as well as the events that led to the force usage. Points that need to be made in these reports are often left out and fail to justify objective reasonableness. They include such phrases, terminology, and content as:

1. The situation was *tense, evolving,* and *uncertain*
2. The situation was *ambiguous*
3. The *suspect* made the force decision for you

Most importantly, the officer should not write as if he knew what level of force he was at when the incident occurred. This is almost impossible to justify considering a dynamic environment and the mere dynamics of force when acting under the color of law.

Some additional concepts that should be considered when writing the report are:

1. Was the officer defending himself or others?
2. Was the officer acting reasonable and prudent?
3. Was the officer within the scope of their employment and jurisdiction?
4. Was the subject being arrested?
5. Was necessary force used?

If any of the above factors are missing, the force used could be excessive or unreasonable. Remember that the only lawful force is necessary force and excessive force begins where necessary force ends. Summarily, the report should be accurate, complete (no gaps), clear, easy to read, concise and objective. It should paint a full picture of what is *relevant*. It should be professional, truthful and provide only the facts and circumstances of the event. A number of good texts on reporting writing are available and can be provided by Looseleaf Law Publications, Inc. Additionally, any training that is offered in report writing should be seriously considered in an effort to learn new and better techniques.

SUMMARY

This chapter has explored various philosophies, perspectives and techniques on training. Specifically, training standards have been defined as statements regarding how a law enforcement or correctional organization views itself in terms of ethics, ideals, morals and principles of carrying out their duty. Standards reflect the best professional practices by providing descriptions of "what" should be accomplished in the police organization and not necessarily "how" they should be doing it. Because the use of force is criticized on a daily basis by citizens and by police administrators, the criticism is often negative in value due to lack of knowledge in the force usage. Based upon the successes and failures of police history and considering the inevitable changes that occur in contemporary society, today's law enforcement officer must be prepared to meet societal threats with the proper response. Furthermore, the police are to effectively work with the community they serve, under undesirable conditions. Training promotes these professional practices through a congruent set of goals, values, and principles that is often recognized through such tasks as report writing, use of force training models, administrative review boards and specific training techniques. Ultimately, training provides a reasonable level of reliability and certainty that is critical to effectively work as a criminal justice practitioner.

QUESTIONS FOR DISCUSSION

1. Explain what stress-based or "scenario-based" training means. Why is it important in the scheme of use of force training?

2. Compare and contrast the principles surrounding control and self-defense techniques. Why should departments utilize these techniques in their training programs?

3. What are at least two issues supporting less-than-lethal technologies and two issues against them as a current strategy in use of force policy and procedure?

4. List the two types of use of force reports that should be completed following a use of force incident. What purpose does each serve?

5. Explain the role of the trainer in a use of force investigation.

REFERENCES

Austen-Kern, L. (2001, May). Training Management Solutions. *The Trainer* pp. 28-43.

City of Canton v. Harris, 489 U.S. 378, 388 (1988).

Commission on Accreditation for Law Enforcement Agencies (1998). *Standards for Law Enforcement Agencies* (4th ed.). Fairfax, VA: CALEA.

Driscoll, M. (1998). *Web-based Training: Using Technology to Design Adult Learning Experiences.* San Francisco, CA: Jossey-Bass/Pfeiffer.

Gilbert, M. J. (1990). Correctional Training Standards: A Basis for Improving Quality and Professionalism. *In Ann Dargis (ed.), State of Corrections: Proceedings of ACA Annual Conferences,* pp. 44-58.

Goldstein, I. L. (1974). *Training.* Monterey, CA: Brooks/Cole Publishing.

Graham v. Connor, 109 S. Ct. 1865 (1989).

Grayson v. Peed, 195 F.3d 692, 696, 697 (4th Cir. 1999).

Holden, R. N. (1994). *Modern Police Management* (2nd ed.). Englewood Cliffs, NJ: Prentice-Hall.

Kansas Law Enforcement Training Center (2001). *Training and Curriculum Guide* [On-line]. Available: www.kletc.org

Law Enforcement and Security Trainers, Inc. (1996). *GRASP Student Manual.* L.E.S.T., Inc.

Lumb, M. (1994). *Professional Standards in Law Enforcement.* New York: McGraw Hill.

O'Rourke, W. J. (1971). Should All Policemen Be College Trained? *The Police Chief, 38 (12).*

Palmiotto, M. J. (1997*). Policing: Concepts, Strategies, and Current Issues in American Police Forces.* Durham, NC: Carolina Academic Press.

Quinones, M. A., & Ehrenstein, A. (1997). *Training for a Rapidly Changing Workplace: Applications of Psychological Research.* Washington, DC: American Psychological Association.

Sapp, A. D., & Carter, D. L. (1992). Police and Higher Education. *In Richard N. Holden, ed., Law Enforcement: An Introduction.* Englewood Cliffs, NJ: Prentice-Hall.

Seaskate, Inc. (1998). *The Evolution and Development of Police Technology.* N.I.J. Grant #95-IJ-CX-Kool (S-3). Washington, D.C.: Office of Justice Programs, U.S. Department of Justice.

Shenkman, F. A. (1984, April). Police Handgun Training and Qualification: A Question of Validity. *FBI Law Enforcement Bulletin,* pp. 7-12.

Stone, A. R., & DeLuca, S. M. (1994). *Police Administration: An Introduction* (2nd ed.). Englewood Cliffs, NJ: Prentice-Hall.

Sullivan, J. L (1971). *Introduction to Police Science.* New York: McGraw Hill.

Tennessee v. Garner, 53 U.S.L.W. 4410 (1985).

Thibault, E. A., Lynch, L. M., & McBride, R. B. (1997). *Proactive Police Management* (4th ed.). Upper Saddle River, NJ: Prentice-Hall.

United States Office of Attorney General (1987). *Report on the Attorney General's Conference on less than Lethal Weapons.* Washington, D.C.: U.S. Department of Justice.

Weisheit, R., Falcone, D., & Wells, L. (1999). *Crime and Policing in Rural and Small Town America.* Prospect Heights, IL: Waveland.

Wills, M. (1998). *Managing the Training Process: Putting the Principles into Practice* (2nd ed.). Brookfield, VT: Gower.

Wilson, O. W. (1963). *Police Administration.* New York: McGraw Hill.

CONCLUSION

Current trends in the field of criminal justice, particularly policing and corrections, require a critical investigation into the use of force. This process becomes a logical cause and effect analysis into how agencies use force, why they use it and how they can do it better. It requires opening the doors to new ideas, examining past problems and working together with a collectivity of individuals to produce the best policy and the best training to lead our officers into the 21st century.

Reminders of the need to create, implement, and enforce variables in force usage are graphically depicted in daily media samples of what are coined "police beatings". While we wince at the headlines, shake our heads in disappointment, and often blame such criticisms on bipartisan politics and special interest group promulgations, officers, trainers and administrators alike must consider and address the fact that law enforcement and correctional officers are public servants. As long as they serve in this capacity, they will be explicitly displayed as community figures, will be watched and will be held accountable in events that lead to charges of deviant behavior.

Considering the aforementioned implications, this book has attempted to provide a theoretical and practical foundation for understanding the use of force and to provide a system of "best practices," utilizing research, principles and philosophies to address the needs of criminal justice practitioners in contemporary society. Two reasons exist for continuous interest in the use of force: safety and integrity. Officers should be able to go home at night, suspects should be able to go to jail, and departments should be free from vicarious liability. Without each, there is little hope in serving the public and serving the public effectively.

Not since the early 1960s has the field of criminal justice been held formally accountable in its use of force under the color of law. And since then, this same field has been subject to severe public scrutiny by not only members of the immediate community but by public officials who also govern these criminal justice agencies. Two levels of public administration must be addressed in governing the use of force: the city and county commissions, and the chiefs and sheriffs who run their individual departments.

At present, there is little cohesion and understanding regarding law enforcement needs, duties, and policies that affect them and the policy and funds that are handed down by the city and county commissions. This failure to acknowledge basic necessities up to and including the legal parameters that govern police use of force place law enforcement administrators and their officers into a precarious position. On the other hand, there are the police administrators who have the resources and tools from their public officials but fail to implement them because of such elements as complacency, fear of change or perhaps a fear of liability. Whatever the reason, the basic premise for teamwork in governing the use of force is the same. Until our governments (at all levels) can identify problems and work together toward a common solution, no progress will be made. The 21st century will be filled with many unknowns in policing as the criminal justice system becomes more dynamic and involved with society. The need for police force will always be evident, and with it will be the need for guidance, learning, and measures of accountability.

Be safe!

Appendix A – Sample Use of Force Policy

As cited in the *Forms* section of this manual, the officer shall use force as appropriated by the **use of force continuum** (*or other model / continuum*). The purpose of any level of force is to *control* the violator by gaining his compliance or to protect the officer or others from harm and is measured by manner, *not* by mechanism. Despite the following protocol of "best practices" listed under federal, state, and administrative guidelines, officers will be required to **use discretion** (based upon training and experience) that is bestowed upon them as law enforcement officers. Ultimately, the officer will be judged by the totality of the circumstances.

An officer must determine what force a *"reasonable officer at the scene"* would have used under the circumstances, without regard to his or her underlying intent or motivation.

Graham v. Connor 109 S.Ct.1865 (1989)

1.   The use of force is not inherently *suspect* or *unlawful.*
2.   There is no legal duty to *retreat* before using force.
3.   You do not need to be *attacked* first before using force.
4.   You do not need to see a weapon first before using force.
5.   No court has ever banned outright any specific technique, tactic or weapon.
6.   Use of deadly force is not limited to any particular tactics and/or techniques to the exclusion of others.
7.   The *best* you use does not have to be the best alternative for resolving the situation, only a *reasonable* one.
8.   You do not have to move up the use of force continuum in a sequential manner.
9.   What you learn about a suspect or situation after force is used may never be used to justify force.
10.   Prior *use* offeree does not necessarily make later uses offeree improper.

LEGAL CITATIONS FOR OFFICER REFERENCE IN USE OF FORCE

U.S. Supreme Court

***Graham v. Connor*: 109 S.Ct. 1865 (1989)**
"whether the officer's use offeree is objectively reasonable in light of the facts and circumstances"

***Tennessee v. Garner*: 105 S.Ct. 1694 (1985)**
"restriction on use of deadly force against fleeing felons"

Federal Court

***Brothers v. Klevenhagen*: 28 F.3d 452 (1994)**
"deadly force not unconstitutional to prevent escape of subject in custody"

***Elliott v. Leavitt*: 99 F.3d 640 (1996)**
"quantity of bullets fired does not prove excessive force"

***Forrett v. Richardson*: 112 F.3d 416 (1997)**
"suspect need not be armed to pose threat of 'serious harm' "

***Mettler v. Whitledge*: 165 F.3d 1197 (1999)**
"tactical guidelines are for protection of officers, not suspects"

***O'Neal v. DeKalb County, GA*: 850 F.2d 653 (1988)**
"no obligation to use minimum amount offeree"

***Reynolds v. County of San Diego*: 858 F.Supp. 1064 (1994)**
"officers don't have to hold fire to see if threatening suspects will actually harm them"

State Court

***People v. Raymond Aguilar, et al.*: 945 P.2d 1204 (1997)**
"hands and feet can constitute deadly force"

Alien v. City of Atlanta, GA: **510 S.E. 2d 64 (1998)**
"target isolation secondary when shooting in self-defense"

In respect to the deadly use of force by members of the (state your agency here):

The police use of force is considered "deadly" if it is "reasonably likely" to cause death.

The offender use of force is considered "deadly" if it is "reasonable likely" to cause serious bodily harm or death.

Vera Cruz v. City of Escondido (CA) 126 F.3d 1214 (1997)

The righteous use of deadly force is:

1. Accurately assessing a suspect's imminent potential for attacking in a life-threatening manner.
2. Accurately articulating why you feared for your life (or someone else's) when you took the action.

The Garner Test: I (from *Tennessee v. Garner, 105 S.Ct. 1694 [1985]*)

Deadly force may be used against a fleeing suspect only if:

- the suspect poses an imminent threat to you or someone else
 or
- you have probable cause to believe he is fleeing from a violent crime

The Garner Test: II

You must have **precluded** other options for preventing his escape.

You must give **warning** you are about to shoot, if **feasible**.

Prohibited Discharge of Firearm

1. The use of firearms is prohibited in the **apprehension** of misdemeanants, since the value to human life far outweighs the gravity of a misdemeanor.
2. Officers shall never use warning shots for any purpose. Warning shots place the lives of innocent bystanders in jeopardy, and in many instances may provoke a suspect into returning fire.
3. Officers shall refrain from firing weapons from a moving vehicle unless the occupants of the other vehicle are using deadly force against the officer by means other than the vehicle, (e.g., shots being fired from both vehicles against the other).

Discharge Regulations

A detailed written report is mandatory on any discharge of firearms. All situations will be thoroughly investigated by the *(state your agency here)* to ascertain if the use of firearms is justified under the circumstances present.

Whenever a member discharges their firearm, either accidentally or in the performance of police duties, they shall verbally notify their on-duty supervisor as soon as time and circumstances permit, but in no event later than the end of their current shift. The member who discharged their firearm shall establish channels with the sheriff, and copies of their report should be submitted to the member's supervisor within the shift during which it occurred.

The lieutenant or undersheriff *(or other administrator)* shall investigate each discharge of firearms personally. After conducting a thorough investigation of the circumstances, the lieutenant or undersheriff shall submit a detailed written report of the results of the conclusions as to whether the discharge was justified and in accordance with this order to the sheriff.

Any member involved in any shooting shall be automatically suspended for a period of not more than ten (10) days until the investigation is complete. If the investigation justifies the shooting, the member shall be compensated his/her regular salary for the time lost.

Use of Force Forms

Members of the *(state your agency here)* that use force must fill out an **Offender/Subject Resistance Form** as denoted by their agency policy manual (see Figure 3.15). This includes but is not limited to: empty-hand control (hard or soft), OC spray, baton, and discharging a firearm. Members of the *(state your agency here)* are not required to complete this form if their weapons (mace, baton, firearms, etc.) are drawn but not used. The immediate availability of weapons (weapons in the "ready" position) in the use offeree continuum is not construed as a *use* of force until the force has actually been delivered.

Index

Tactical Attitude
Learn from Powerful Real-Life Experience!
Includes *Officer Survival Creed* (Suitable for framing)
by Phil L. Duran & Dennis Nasci

Path of the Warrior
An Ethical Guide to Personal & Professional Development in the Field of Criminal Justice
by Larry F. Jetmore

The COMPSTAT Paradigm
Management Accountability in Policing, Business and the Public Sector
by Vincent E. Henry, CPP, Ph.D.

How to Really, *Really* Write Those Boring Police Reports
by Kimberly Clark

The New Age of Police Supervision and Management
A Behavioral Concept
by Michael A. Petrillo & Daniel R. DelBagno

Effective Police Leadership
Moving Beyond Management
by Thomas E. Baker, Lt. Col. MP USAR (Ret.)

21st Century Policing
Community Policing
by Sgt. Steven Rogers

Domestic Violence Survival Guide
by Cliff Mariani

(800) 647-5547   **www.LooseleafLaw.com**

Notes on *Your* Department's Force Policy

Notes on *Your* Department's Force Policy

_____

_____

_____

_____

_____

_____

_____

_____

_____

_____

_____

_____

_____

_____

_____

_____

_____

_____

_____

_____

_____